Argument

in the

Railroad conspiracy case

entitled

the People of Michigan

vs.

Abel F.Fitch and others.

Tried before his honor,Warner Wing,
presiding judge,of the Circuit
court for the county of Wayne,
at the May term,1851
in the city of
Detroit

Detroit
Duncklee,Wales & co.
1851

ARGUMENT

OF

JAMES A. VAN DYKE, ESQ.,

ON THE SO CALLED

RAILROAD CONSPIRACY CASE.

THE PEOPLE OF MICHIGAN vs. ABEL F. FITCH AND OTHERS.

MR. VAN DYKE:

TUESDAY, September 15, 1851, 8 A. M.

The Court being in session, JAMES A. VAN DYKE, Esq., counsel for the Prosecution, addressed the Jury as follows:

May it please the Court, and Gentlemen of the Jury: I cannot refrain from congratulating you that the long and wearisome investigation in which you are engaged, is so near to its close. Many months since, before the leaves were green or the flowers had bloomed, ere the spring time had departed, and while our hopes and feelings moved in sympathy with the gladdening freshness which the season shed around us, you were summoned from your homes, comforts, business and pleasures, to assume a serious responsibility, in aid of the administration of justice. Since then, while we have associated together, and day by day discharged, I trust with patience and fidelity, our toilsome, but solemn duties, time has run its ceaseless course; the summer came with all its joy and brightness—it, too, has faded away, and already the crimson leaves of the forest warn us that autumn is passing its withering fingers over the face of Nature.

I indulge in this thought because it induces the mind to reflect upon our own condition, and the vanity of acting otherwise than under a deep sense of duty. Most of us have reached the middle age.

—*our* spring time has departed—*our* summer has almost left us—*our* autumn is nigh, and ere long the descending snows of winter will fall upon our heads. All things teach the dread truth that "life is fleeting," and that we should move through its mazy paths of cares and pleasures, with hope and vision fixed on the eternity which lies beyond.

In this case, gentlemen, we have each a solemn duty to perform—let us discharge it with a high sense of the responsibility which rests upon us.

In the views which I am about submit to you, I will earnestly endeavor to treat this cause with the seriousness its importance demands, and with the candor and fairness due to you and to the Court.

While I feel pleased in beholding the laurels which this trial has en twined around other brows, I will seek to gather none for my own. will neither wander into the paths of fancy, nor address myself to those who sit *without* the jury box. I will remember, however dull it may render me,that my duty confines me to *this* cause, I will speak *only* of it, and address myself *only to you.* I will pass over the case gentleman, as nearly as possible in the same order which has been pursued by the distinguished counsel who last addressed you for the defence. I shall not seek or hope to leave the impress of oratorical power upon your imagination, but trust, ere I conclude, to convince your reason, that *every* point urged by the defence is fallacious, and without foundation in the facts and evidence before you.

An objection of a technical character has been interposed by the counsel for the prisoners, which I propose briefly to allude to before his Honor, the Judge.

The Court is aware, that at common law, an accessory could only be indicted and tried by one of two ways, viz: *with* the principal—the jury first passing on the principal's guilt: or secondly, after the conviction or outlawry of the principal—the record of his conviction affording *prima facie* evidence of his guilt.

It being found that this rule of the common law did not operate to the furtheranee of justice, but rather to the shielding of guilt, the Act of 7 Geo. 4, C. 64, was passed to remedy the evil.

This Act retained the two common law modes of trial of accessories before the fact, and provided a third, viz: as, and for a substantive felony; and this act is substantially and, indeed, almost literally re-enacted in and by our own Rev. Stat. 1846, P. 686, Chap. 161, Sec. 2, which is as follows:

"Every person who shall counsel, hire, or otherwise procure any felony to be committed, may be indicted and convicted as an accessory before the fact, either with the principal felon, or after the conviction of the principal felon, or he may be indicted or convicted of a substantive felony, whether the principal felon *shall or shall not be amenable to justice,* and in the last mentioned case, may be punished in the same manner as if convicted of being accessory before the fact."

The present indictment counts as follows, viz: 1st. Against all as principals in the arson of the Depot. 2nd. Against George W. Gay as principal in the arson. 3d. Against the other defendants as accessories before the fact.

Since the finding of the indictment, and after the arraignment and plea of Gay and of all the other defendants, Gay died, and the prisoner's counsel now submit, that although the indictment was well and valid up to the time of the death of said deceased, yet on the occurrence of that event, it became incompetent to proceed thereunder against others of the prisoners as accessories. The objection stated seems to be, that these prisoners are not indicted for a substantive felony, but under the common law form and rule along with the principal, and that he dying, the objection becomes valid.

I do not propose, at this stage of proceedings, to discuss the subject at length, because a Court will not here arrest the trial, or prevent the finding of the jury, unless for conclusive reason. After all the expense involved and time consumed—after the postponement of the objection to almost the close of the case—the verdict, which may dispose of the whole matter, should not unnecessarily be prevented, especially as, if adverse, the prisoners can have the benefit of their objection by distinct motion to the Court.

The learned counsel in support of their objection cite, 1st, A precedent of an indictment for substantive felony, from Archibald's Crim. Pl. 2nd, A text from Russell on Crimes. 3d, The Queen vs. Ashmall & Tay., 9 C. and P., p. 236. The precedent and text from Russell require no examination. The case from C. & P. appears to sanction the general idea of the counsel here, though not to the full extent claimed. It is a *nisi prisi* case. It does not appear to be regarded or cited afterwards as an authority. The objection of Carrington for defendant, was that the name of the principal should not have been given. The subsequent case of Regina vs. Caspar and others, 9 C. & P. 289, shows that in an indictment against accessories, the principal felon *shall be named*, and it, with the still later case, 9 C. & P. 555, shows the unsubstantial character of the objection. The more recent case of the Queen vs. Wallace & Wallace, 41 E. C. L. 113, is quite in point.—The indictment had a distinct count against Loose as principal, and proceeded to charge said defendants as accessories before the fact *in continuation of the same count.* Loose had not been tried, was not upon trial, and had not been outlawed. The defendants Wallace were upon trial; this distinct objection was taken; over-ruled by the *nisi prius* judge; the objection reserved for the opinion of the fifteen Judges, who held the conviction correct, and the prisoners were sentenced.

Again, I claim that the offence of burning a depot was not a common law offence, and that under the peculiar language of our Statute* it is doubtful and unsettled whether our Courts will hold it to be strictly a felony. Hence all the defendants may be guilty as principals for a misdemeanor under the first count, there being no accessories to misdemeanors, and all who would be accessories to felony, being principals in misdemeanor. The Court would on this ground alone, decline now to stop the trial.

But I insist further, that the third count in this indictment is a good count against the defendants for a substantive felony, and that it merely refers to the preceding count for a particular description of the offence. 2. That if it is not, the defect is formal, not substantial—"does not tend to the prejudice of the defendants," and is therefore cured by Sec. 34, p. 700, Rev. Stat, 1846. 3. That the above cases cited from the E. C. L. Reports, together justify the sustaining the indictment in its present form. 4. That even at Common Law the accessory could be legally tried *by his own consent without and before* his principal. Chit. Crim. Law, 219.

In the case of Ashmall & Tay, relied upon by defendants above cited, the objection was taken *before plea*, that the defendant was not *compellable* to plead to the indictment.

In the case at bar the prisoners object *too late*. They have pleaded to the indictment, have proceeded after the principal's death, and put themselves on their defence, thereby signifying consent, and have actually consented in writing, to proceed after Gay's death. It is therefore humbly submitted for these reasons, that this Court will not now entertain or sustain the objection, but permit the case to go before and be passed upon by the jury.

Gentlemen of the Jury, while in some respects I rejoice, in others I regret that we are here to-day. I rejoice that although during the long period we have spent together, death has swept away some connected with this trial--that although disease has at times visited you or your families, yet that God in his providence has, amid your prolonged and arduous cares, preserved you in health and vigor to discharge the high duty you owe to them and your country. I am glad that we can here apply our minds to the calm investigation of truth; that while the Sun of Heaven lights up our beloved city, and sheds its radiance upon the fields and forests and beautiful river within our vision, we can sit free from the excitements of life, and with an eye single to the ends of law and justice, and devote our best energies to the necessary, though laborious task of a fair and candid examination of the mass of evidence which has accumulated in this cause. I regret, on your account, that the responsibility of a decision has fallen upon you, and for myself that it has devolved upon me to say ought about these unfortunate prisoners, yet they are duties that may not be passed by or put aside. That you will discharge your duty in justice, though tempered with mercy, I have no doubt. I would, gentlemen, that I could perform mine as well. You must expect from me, gentlemen, no eloquent declamations, for I will frame no dazzling theories upon a misrepresentation or perversion of the testimony, whether accidental or designed. I will not weave a single wreath of fancy, but will seek to bind your minds and my own to the plain and unadorned truths that are apparent in this case, and which alone should influence you. Although I have to follow in the wake of elaborately prepared and eloquent speeches, I wlll not seek to emulate them. I will neither quote *Latin*, or decorate my periods by selections from the classic pages of Addison; nor will I follow the counsel through his terrible phillipic upon the leading witness of the prosecution, which I fear lost much of its force upon minds familiar with the strangely similar portraiture of Junius drawn in the "Vision of Judgment." But while I refrain from pursuing the meteoric fancies, eloquent phillippics, and sublime apostrophes to the "sainted dead," which have shed a false though brilliant light upon the dark details of crime revealed to you day by day, I will go through the case fairly and discuss it fully. I will "nothing extenuate, nor aught set down in malice. I will base my arguments upon the testimony, not as I *would have it*, but *as it is*. I will speak, not to the world, *but to you*, who can correct and hold me in judgment, if I fail to redeem the promises of fairness and candor which I make. Heaven can witness for me that I desire no fame at the expense of these unfortunate men. I will use no bitter words; I will affect no bitter loathing; I will assail neither man, woman or child, except under the urgent pressure of duty and necessity. I wish I could be spared the painful task of doing so at all. During our labors death has visited some of those who awaited your judgement—it is to be regretted. By none was it more lamented than by myself and the gentlemen associated with me for the prosecution. I hoped that respect for the inscrutable decrees of Providence, would have sealed all lips upon that sad occurrence. If it had rested with the prosecution, the dead, however guilty, would have been suffered to slumber in silence. Neither you nor I could close our eyes to the solemn fact that "those who were, are not." Death was in our midst, and though silence might veil its horrors, like the skeleton at the Egyptian feast, its unseen presence was felt by all.—But for no purpose, for no end, not even to convict the guilty, would the prosecution have invaded the tomb, and dragged the image of its lifeless tenant before you, either for unseemly invective or scarcely less seemly panegyric. The counsel for defendants have judged otherwise—it has seemed to them wise and proper to tear aside the veil that divides the living from the dead, and to invoke the "sainted spirit" of the leader of these defendants—a phantom, gentlemen, that I know will fail in the design of frightening you from your propriety, but the invocation of which entails on me in certain portions of my argument, the painful duty of speaking of the dead and their deeds, in terms which I would fain use only of the living. It would be unseemly to seek occasion to probe the deeds and motives of those who are no longer of this world, but it would be criminal weakness to shrink from the task when duty demands its performance.

Much, far too much, has been said to you, gentlemen, about excitement. However pleasing and eloquent all this may have been, like too many of the *arguments* urged upon you, they "will not bide the test." Excitement! where is it gentlemen? Surely not here. Whom does it influence? Surely not you. Examine this "excitement" upon which such impassioned appeals have been made. What is it? Four months since, thirty or forty men, charged with atrocious crimes were arrested and brought to our city. The crime with which they stood charged was one that touched us nearly. It had threatened to reduce our young and beauteous city, to a mass of black and smouldering ashes, and to entomb in its ruins, properties that were the reward of long and ceaseless toil. Charged with this fearful crime they came among us in irons, and surrounded by every moral evidence of guilt. It was natural that for a time, the public pulse should beat the quicker, and so it did, but there was no attempt at violence; there was no desire that the accused should meet ought bnt a fair and impartial trial, and almost before they were lodged in our jail, the excitement their arrival created was again hushed, and the pulse of our peaceful and law-abiding city again beat with its wonted tranquility;

and as you well know, during the greater portion of this trial, but for the crowd of witnesses, the little room in which we pursued our investigations would not have been one-third full. Excitement! Among whom? Where in two hours a Jury was tried and empannelled, each member of it a resident of this city—this hot-bed of excitement—and each member of it equally acceptable to the prosecution and the prisoners. *Dangerous* excitement! It is a foul, and though I love not harsh words, a false stigma upon our city. Where could these prisoners have had a fairer trial or more indulgence extended to them? Where else in a city filled with able counsel, unengaged by the government, would the prosecution have delayed the trial, at great sacrifice, merely that counsel might be procured for prisoners, from a distance of hundreds of miles? Where, before, has such freedom of defence been suffered? Where before, have the rules of law been waived by the prosecution, that the defence might introduce all that could be found to militate against the character of an important witness? In what other instance has counsel for defence, without check or interruption, been suffered in an address to the jury, to comment upon testimony stricken from the case—to travel over the history of the country, and read unsworn letters as evidence? In the whole range of criminal reports no case can be found in which such liberal indulgence has been extended in aid of the defence of prisoners.

Much has been said to you about public opinion; but what have you or I to do with it? It cannot, and it should not, influence us. The streets may be filled with rumors and conjectures; but we are not in the streets, and such things float past us unregarded. We are in a building, for the present at least, consecrated to the administration of Justice; we are gathered at its shrine—if not a holy, a solemn one; and excitement and public opinion should both be banished from the elements that surround it. If strong public opinion exists, it is not the creation of the prosecution; and it is unjust, by implication or otherwise, to charge it upon us. If the City Press, for a time, published news in connection with this trial, that it deemed important to the public, it has long ceased to do so. If this much-talked-of public opinion exists, who made it? Not the prosecution; its lips have been uniformly closed by a sense of propriety. And I would ask those who address such language to you—Have the prosecuting counsel run through the streets, pledging their honors to the innocence or guilt of the prisoners? Have they sought, day after day, to raise an influence that might be brought to bear upon your deliberations? Have they sown distrust broadcast in the community, or gathered public meetings for the purpose of denouncing these judicial proceedings? Have they got up death-bed scenes to affect the imagination of women and children; for I presume they were scarcely designed to influence men? Have they published *sermons* of doubtful morality and perverted taste, for distribution, with reports of Supervisors, comments of the Press, and fancy scenes by youthful and ardent counsel, annexed? Have they done aught but their duty, or done that aught but fairly? Have they passed through the streets, stating that they knew, and could wager, that certain of the jury, they might name, would never agree to convict? No, gentlemen, the prosecution do no such things, and *"laugh to scorn"* those who do. They know *you;* they have faith in your intelligence and integrity, and await with patience and respect the result of your judgment. They know you, and despise the childish weakness which seeks, by such shallow courses, to "tnrn awry" the even justice of your deiiberations.

We are here to seek your verdict by no such means; we are here to discuss testimony, and, aided by lights of past ages, and the wisdom and experience of our respected Judge, to separate truth from falsehood. You have heard this testimony; you have listened to it with unwearying patience; you will soon retire, "the world forgetting," though not by it forgot, with your responsibilities gathered upon yourselves, to make up your verdict according to that law which has been well styled "the perfection of human reason," and which, however eloquently it may be assailed, even by its own disciples, who serve and minister at its shrine, bears stamped upon its venerable front, the sanction of ages, of sages, and of worlds—willing, if you can, to acquit these men; but ready, also, if your judgment and the law direct it, to find them guilty.

Permit me to call your attention for a single moment to the subject of bail, about which so much has been said to you. It is true that with the matter of bail you have nothing to do; the propriety of requiring bail, and the amount at which it is fixed, is exclusively a question for the Court. It cannot enter into your deliberations, or form any portion of the ingredients from which you are to extract your verdict; and the same may be truly said of many other topics upon which you have been eloquently addressed. Yet as the prosecution has been assailed in relation to this question, both out of court and in it; as it was the foundation of a highly wrought and elaborate appeal to you, you will admit the propriety of my saying a few words in relation to it. Why the eminent counsel should have addressed you upon this subject I am at a loss to conceive. I can scarce believe he would pay you so poor a compliment, or that his own judgment would be so much at fault, as to suppose you such men as even his acknowledged power could seduce from the path of duty you are sworn to tread, or deceive into the fabrication of a verdict upon a matter that is is in no sense submitted to you.

A case of *supposed* oppression is a tempting field for the display of rhetorical powers, and did I possess the fluent tongue of the eminent counsel, I too might be tempted to create a field suited to my taste, abandon the dry details of this case, and sport "fancy free" around it.

If the oppression and tyrany described in relation to bail did actualy exist, sympathy with its victims would be an emotion natural to the human breast, and it would naturally become the chosen theme of the conscious orator, but even then, gentlemen, to it, you would have nothing to say. Laws which we ourselves have framed, and which we have not yet deemed fit to alter, has vested the decision of such questions not in you, but in the court; those who disapprove of that law —as undoubtedly they have a right to disapprove, should address themselves not to jurors sworn to administer law *as it is*, but to such popular assemblies as can influence a revision of the obnoxious statute.

But again gentlemen, does this tyranny and oppression really exist, or is it

——"a false creation
Proceeding from the heat oppressed brain?"

You will readily concede that persons suspected of crime should be arrested when the evidence of guilt is *fair and reasonable.* If arrests were only made when guilt was a matter of absolute certainty, they could never be made at all, for guilt is certain, only after conviction. Then, there was no oppression in arresting the prisoners.

If a Grand Jury after careful investigation thinks proper to present an indictment in the form prescribed by law, you will concede there is no great oppression in saying that the accused should be submitted to the ordeal of a trial. But how ensure a trial? If left at liberty the guilty conscience would prompt to flight, the guiltless alone would abide the issue, and courts would be engaged in the constant trial of innocent persons. There is no alternative left but to confine the accused, or require bail in such amount as will ensure his presence at the final ordeal.

The system of bail is not after all the instrument of oppression but one of the great safeguards of society—converting the trial of criminals from chance to reasonable certainty.

But we are told the bail demanded is exhorbitant. The amount of bail fixed is large, but it is fixed as it should be, with reference to the enormity of the crime charged—the circumstances of the prisoners—and the inducements that would lead them to flee from justice. The prisoners differ widely in worldly circumstances—the more wealthy could more easily find bail in a large amount—their social position too would involve a greater motive to escape conviction—and therefore a wisely exercised discretion has varied the amount of bail required, in accordance with the individual circumstances and position of the prisoners. The object of bail is not to fix a price upon the avoidance of a trial, and thus compromise with crime. Here where the laws are mild but strictly and impartially administered is not the place where "offence's gilded hand may shove by justice." The design of bail is to secure the presence of the accused. No more has been required in this case. I beg you gentlemen to let your recollections revert to the time when this question of bail was legitimately debated before this Court, though in your presence—and without knowing your opinions, ask, with confidence; did you then think it was exhorbitant? If you did not think so then, why should you think so now? Surely not, because you then heard it calmly discussed before his Honor, and since fervidly before yourselves. You will remember that it was stated that the defendants could furnish any amount of bail; persons so vaunting, and charged with one of the highest offences known to the law, should be held to bail in no light sum. Interesting calculations have been placed before you, and you have been shown by figures "which never lie" but which I confess have *sometimes* deceived me, that the bail required, swelled up to an enormous sum and perhaps it does, but it does so by process ofmultiplication. The fact that there are forty defendants, does not lessen the character of the guilt of each one nor should the complicity reduce the amount of each individual's bail. It would follow therefore, that the aggregate amount of bail would be forty times as great as that required if there was but a single defendant, a result that does not indicate oppression but which in the hands of an ingenious mathematician produces very high sounding figures.

I will waste no more of your time upon this subject; it is the same which was duly considered and calmly decided in an early stage of this trial. It has been resuscitated and brought before you surrounded by heated invectives against "corporations," but as corporations chance to be governed by the same law as individuals, and are entitled to the same protecting care, I confess I fail to perceive that even this new ingredient makes out the case of "tyranny and oppression."

Again and again you are told that Death has visited and thinned the ranks of these unfortunate men; and the corse and its shroud are seized upon as fit pictures to disturb your visions, in the hope apparently of making you shudder as you gaze. And because Providence has deemed it fit to remove two of these defendants, shall we be told in deliberate argument, that you are therefrom to infer the innocence of those who are left! Is such to be the basis of a solemn verdict?

Permit me to ask you gentlemen—what have you to do with deathbed scenes—false in fact, morbid in taste, and wholly irrelevant to this issue? You will I am sure, entirely dismiss from your *imaginations*, these ghostly fancies, which your good sense has doubtless prevented from finding lodgment in your *minds*.

But the picture is afancied scene—destitute even of the merit of simple truth. The dying words, which are now so sought to be perverted, were in fact of far different import; and were flung off from a fevered brain amid the fearful delirium of deathly collapse, and let me say, dressed up as they now are, they would meet from the deceased, could he hear them, no sign of recognition—naughtbut the smile of derision. They might serve to adorn the page of some yellow covered novel—they have served to grace two elegant perorations—but they scarcely seem appropriate in the argument of a trial of such magnitude and importance. I regret that the last delirious moments of the dead should be the subject of public comment; but as counsel on the other side have thought otherwise, it is my duty to follow them with the truth, and it will be the duty of the Court to tell you to banish them from your minds, if perchance they linger there.

Gentlemen, you have been gravely told, that "you stand between the living and the dead," that "the lightest error in your finding, will prove a source of constant remorse," that "the thought should make you tremble." If this indeed be true,you may well tremble. Uncertainty and imperfection are stamped uhon earth, and upon Man, *its* choicest production,and upon *his* proudest efforts. Feeble man talking of certainty! His loftiest fabrics crumble beneath the step of time; or are crushed or scattered before an hours' breath. His cultivated intellect—his glowing mind—lie shattered and quenched in a moment's space. No gentlemen, no such fearful responsibility rests on you—no such unerring certainty is required of you—and if he who seeks to grasp or attain such perfection, will only realize how

"Vaunting ambition doth o'er leap itself."

Neither reason law or sense requires from you the exercise of superhuman attributes. You are bound to exercise caution, care, and deliberation—to weigh the evidence with your best judgmen—to sift it with your keenest penetration; and having done this, to state honestly the convictions of your minds—no more and no less.

In this connection, I beg to call your attention to the following passage, found in pages 386 and 7 of Cowen & Hill's notes to Phillip's Evidence, and which is a portion of a charge delivered to a jury. It will have more effect on you than any language of counsel and will explain away the sophistry that seeks to engender fears and doubts in your mind.

"It has often been said by counsel that Jurors in rendering a verdict *swear* that the prisoner is guilty or not guilty. The Jury swear to no such thing; they declare in rendering a verdict the result of the conviction of their minds from the evidence produced, having previously sworn to give a true verdict according to the evidence."

Speaking of the extreme cases so often cited before Jurors the same learned aothor says:

"The plain, practical rules of evidence established for ages should not be shaken by such collections of cases in the works of theoretical writers. Such cases may be inserted to induce greater caution in jurors; but if employed for any other purpose, their application in the generality of cases depending on circumstantial evidence is dangerous in the extreme."

[The learned counsel read several other passages from the same author, to the effect that jurors, even though they sometimes erred, were not accountable for more than a wise and careful exercise of their judgment, and then proceeded:]

Gentlemen, in this case, I cherish no resentment. I feel no wound. My breast bleeds from no poisoned shaft. My heart harbors no other feeling than kindness to all concerned, and most happy would I feel, if consistently with duty, I might avoid saying a single word that could bear a personal applicatication to counsel or others. But the stern dictates of duty compel me to say that the learned counsel who has preceded me, has argued to you upon a false basis—whether it was the result of accident or design, it is not for me to insinuate. But it is for me *now* to say, and hereafter to *show* to your entire satisfaction, that you have not been frankly dealt with. The testimony was presented to you, through a false and discolored medium. After the announcement made several days since, by one of the counsel for defence, that their entire time, from almost the commencement of this case, had been occupied in making extracts, analysises, codifications, and tables of the testimony, which would be presented for your consideration by his distinguished associate. I did expect that matter, so laboriously and elaborately prepared, would have been characterized by at least some show of fairness and candor. Has it been? The coloring of testimony is one of the most frequent errors of counsel; where this arises from warm and hasty discussion, it is excusable—for it is natural that the mind heated by debate and recalling the evidence, by the sole aid of fallible memory, should lend to it the tinge and hue of its own warm hopes and feelings. But whether the same charitable excuse can be extended to written tables and extracts—"cold inanimate matter"—compiled line by line and figure by figure, by the sun's bright beam, and the lamp's glimmer, it is not for me to say; but it is free for you to judge. If the fervent zeal of counsel has led them unconsciously into this error, far be it from me to censure them, or do more than correct their mistakes. The office of advocate is one of the highest trust and confidence. In no other relation of life does man place all that he can love and cherish so entirely in the hands of his fellow; and he is unfit to discharge its sacred duties, who has not zeal, and sympathy, and ardor sufficient at times, amid the hot excitement of argument to lead him even into errors. Faults thus arising, partake largely of the characteristics of virtue; they spring from the same source as our holiest emotions, our best and gentlest feelings hang around them in graceful drapery; and though duty might compel me to remove the veil, I would do it gently, and not with a ruthless hand.

But it is different when these errors spring not from impassioned ardor, but from midnight study. In the latter case, they should arm jurors with a degree of suspicion, but of all this, you will have to judge. It is mine to tell you that the testimony has been unfairly stated to you, and that almost every point taken by the learned counsel, has been erected upon a misstatement of the evidence. I am conscious gentlemen, that this is a bold statement; and that if I fail to maintain its truth, it will react upon the prosecution. But if you follow me carefully as I review the argument of the counsel, and read the testimony in connection—not from *manuscript* extracts, but from the printed evidence which many of you hold in your hands, I have no fear that you will deem I have overstepped the bounds of truth.

After disposing of some other preliminary remarks of counsel, I will call your attention back to the points urged in connection with the evdence.

The learned counsel has solemnly informed you that this *is* Detroit—a proposition based upon truth, and to the entire accuracy of which, I am thrice happy to assent.

He has further informed you that upon the line of the Central Rail Road there are some humble hamlets constituting Leoni; that fifteen years since, the Legislature of this State, commenced the construction of a great thoroughfare, which passed through that same town of Leoni; that its agents were kind to the people, and the peaceful occupants of this "*small district*" reciprocated the feeling; no cattle were killed; the engine and its train passed safely by—and no murmur of complaint disturbed the quiet harmony of the scene; that in an evil hour, the State forgetting what was due to herself and the people, sold the road to a heartless and greedy Corporation—then the scene was changed—tyranic agents frowned—cattle were killed; complaint was followed by imprecation--and amid the humble hamlets of Leoni, was commenced a struggle—which in a form of justice, a grave and distinguished Senator tells us "can have but one end in a country where jealousy of corporate power can never be suppressed."

Such, gentlemen, is the fancy sketch drawn for you by the defence. It is simply *untrue;* but you must permit me to tender my meed of admiration to the luxuriant imagination that could paint such a scene from such materials, one so gently beautiful—so unique-- so totally unlike any thing that was ever seen or dreamt of round "the *rural* districts of Leoni."

Gentlemen, the true history of the road tells an entirely different tale; that from the hour when the first locomotive left this City, down to the hour when the State sold her interest to this Corporation, there was nothing but trouble and heart-burnings from this very cause; and in this very town of Leoni, that among the very first who raised the cry of complaint and hostility, was Abel F. Fitch; and that the seeds of enmity which have since ripened into such bitter fruit were planted and had sprung to goodly growth, even while the road was still managed by "the kind and gentle agents of the State."

I tell you as a matter of history, that the Company has, in respect to cattle killed, pursued the same policy as did the State. I will show you the truth of this, and then you will judge of the consistency of eulogizing the one and denouncing the other. When the late Mr. Wells was Superintendant, the State refused to pay for cattle killed; afterwards, perhaps, as *elections* approached, it did pay for awhile, but soon found it was creating a cattle market at every crossing on the track; that to pay for such *accidents (?)* would drain the entire revenue of the road; and the old and only true policy was adopted. I will read you a sentence from the Report of the Board of Internal Improvement made in 1845, while the road was still managed by the State, and then tell me if it is I or the counsel who paints your fancy scenes? I refer to Joint Documents of 1846, No. 4:

"The amount paid for killing and maiming cattle is becoming enormously large. If animals are allowed to run upon our tracks, very many must inevitably be killed; and when no want of care on the part of the engineer be proven, should not the loss fall *entirely* upon the owner of the property destroyed." "If the owner is not debarred from collecting any portion of the loss, should he not at least share in the risk, say to the amount of one half of the damage?" Such was the policy of the State, and the latter and kindlier of the above suggestions has been the policy of the Company; and the people along the line, save only in Leoni, have generally acquiesced in it.

What has been the history of the road while in the hands of the State? For years it dragged its slow length along; an incumbrance and a burthen. The State needed engines, cars, depots—every material to prosecute or sustain with energy or profit, this important work; but its credit was gone, and it was immersed in debt. Our population was thinly scattered across the entire breadth of the Peninsula. Engines dragged slowly and heavily through the dense forests. Our City numbered but 12,000 people; our State was destitute of wealth; our farmers destitute of markets; our laborers destitute of employment; and so far as the interests of the State and her people were identified with the Railroad, itpresent ed a joyless present, a dark and frowning future.

In a fortunate hour, the State sold the road, and the millions of this denounced Company, were flung broadcast through our community; they took up the old track, relaid a better one, extended the road to the extreme line of the State—laid down at enormous cost; over 400 miles of fences to guard the property of all, save those who wanted a beef market at each crossing; multiplied the accommodation seven-fold —quadrupled the speed—increased traffic and commerce, so that while in 1845, the State passed 26,000 tons over the road; in 1850 the Company passed 134,000 tons; created markets for our products, snatched the tide of passing emigration, from the hands of a steam-boat monopoly, hostile to Michigan, and threw it unto the heart of our State, until now, where heaven's light was once shut out by dense forests, it shines over fertile fields, and rich, luxuriant harvests, and the rivers of our State, which once ran with wasteful speed to the bosom of the Lakes, turn the machinery which renders our rich products available. With them Capital made its home amongst us, our credit was restored—hope and energy sprung from their lethargic sleep, labor clapped her glad hands and shouted for joy; and Michigan bent for the moment, like a sappling by the fierceness of a passing tempest; relieved from the debts and burthens, rose erect, and in her youthful strength, stood proudly up among her sister States.

Who shall stop this glorious work, which is spreading blessings and prosperity around us? Who shall dare to say, "thus far shalt thou go and no farther?" Who shall dictate to it after doing so much? Must it now pause and rest in inglorious ease? No, gentlemen, it shall not be stayed; it shall speed onward in triumph; it shall add link after link to the great chain that binds mankind together; it *shall* speed onward, still onward—through the gorges of the mountain—over the depths of the valley, till the Iron Horse, whose bowels are fire—"out of whose nostrils goeth forth smoke," and "whose breath kindleth coals," shall be heard thundering through the echoing solitudes of the Rocky Mountains, startling the live Indian from his wild retreat, and ere long reaching the golden shores of the far off Pacific, there to be welcomed by the glad shouts of American freemen at the glorious event which has conquered time and distance, and bound them by nearer chords to older homes and sister States.

A detestable Monopoly! These railroads built by united energies and capital, are the great instruments in the hand of God to hasten onward the glorious mission of Religion, and Civilization. Already is our Central Road stretching forth its hands, and giving assurance that soon shall its iron track reach across the neighboring Provinces from Detroit to Niagara; and that ere long the scream of the locomotive shall be heard over the sound of the cataract—which shall thunder forth in deafening peals, that glorious event. Our brethren on the shores of the Atlantic, with whom we are bound by every interest, association and affection, will hail the shortened tie with ardent welcome.

Beneath the beneficial influence of Companies like this, space is annihilated; weeks are reduced to the compass of days, and in spite of the wicked purposes of bad men, this and kindred Companies shall continue to spread and contribute to the greatness and prosperity of our country, until the earth vibrates with the pulses of her glory.

But Leoni is a "*a rural district.*" It is one of the oldest settled towns of the State; but its statistical history tells a strange story of its progress, and gives a sad incident of its welfare. While a vast tide of emigration has poured itself into our State; while forests have become fenced and cultivated farms—rural districts, populous ones—villages, towns and cities—in every other part of the State; in Leoni—this place of "hamlets," and "refuge of virtue"—the population has decreased—its population in 1850 being less than in 1845; a significant fact, gentlemen, and one that indicates that, if it is "a rural district" now, it will be still more emphatically a *rural* district ten years hence, unless a better and more law-abiding spirit takes up its abode in the hearts of that community. The truth of this anomaly in the statistical history of our State, will be found in "Munger's Landmarks,' and other statistical tables.

But, gentlemen, you are told the Railroad Company employed spies; and, in the hope to rouse your prejudice, a fierce denunciation has been poured forth against them. 'Tis true that, at the close of his remarks, counsel tried to spread a little sweetness over the poison he had scattered; but, gentlemen, you nor I cannot soon forget the bitter terms in which these men were assailed. We cannot forget the language used, or that such men as Mr. Van Arman, Mr. Clark, Taylor, Hudson, Faulkner, Rogers, were named, and held up with every term of obloquy, as spies, unworthy of credit. Of Mr. Clark, who, I perceive, is not present, I may say a passing word. It may seem wise to counsel; the spasms of a hopeless defence may demand an attempt to fling odium over the fair fame of a good and worthy man; but he who wantonly assails Darius Clark, in this community, is mistaken, and will find, in the end, that his bitter speeches, like Arab curses,

"Still come home to roost."

Gentlemen, there is not, in our entire State, a man better known, more loved, or more respected, than Mr. Clark. Kindly in disposition, courteous in demeanor, and possessed of a high order of abilities, his fellow-citizens have again and again conferred on him offices of the highest trust; but lives there a man who can say he has discharged them with aught save honor to himself, and benefit to his fellow-citizens? His home is surrounded by friends who love and admire him; and I fear that the bitter words of the counsel will grate harshly on many an ear. I submit to you, gentlemen, that imputations of discredit cast upon such a man—a gentleman of high character and position, and of unblemished reputation—are both improper and unwise; and that counsel who became such unjust assailants, forget

"That he of old, who struck the oak,
Dreamed not of the rebound."

But it is said others were employed who do not stand so fair and high; even so, gentlemen; I am still too obtuse to perceive the impropriety of employing them to find out the guilty perpetrators of these outrages, nay more, I think the duty of so doing was due by the company to the community, even more than to itself.

Let me recall your minds to the outrages on this road. What was its state? What would have been its proba le fate had criminal inaction marked its management?

Whether sitting in your homes or attending to your business, you must have herad that the passage over it had become dangerous—that in consequence travel was almost diverted from it. It is a matter of public notoriety, that the company was compelled to stop running a night train, as to do so, endangered the lives of passengers. Engine after engine was flung from the track—bullet after bullet whistled round the engine house, till the passage of Leoni, "the rural district," became one of peril and danger, and the engineer who passed in safety returned thanks to Providence. Under such circumstances what was the company to do? Arm men? take the law into their own hands, and shoot down aggressors along the line of the road? Were they to rest until hundreds of lives were sacrificed? until the line of the road was made desolate and waste, and the soil of Leoni was enriched by the mangled bodies of our citizens? Ask yourselves the question, gentlemen; would you have entrusted yourselves or your families, over that road in the night time? You know you would not. Under such circumstances it was not only a right, it became an imperative and solemn duty to use the most effectual means to arrest the work of devastation, and stay the crime stained hands of those who would murder, not by units, nor by tens, but by hhndreds. In the language of one equally eminent for talents and virtues, "if in her whole wide armory, justice had but one weapon that could pierce the aggressors, they were bound to use it." It was a duty they owed to the public, and for the non-performance of which they would have been held strictly to account, Had this company failed to use the only effectual made of bringing guilt to light or punishment, what would have been the result. Limb and life *were* perilled, they would *have been* lost. Our State would have been disgraced. Already travellers, under the salutaroy warning of handbills, braved the passage of the lakes in the most stormy season, rather than the still more perilous passage of Leoni, and soon our lovely Peninsula, branded by crimes more fearful than any that have yet marked the history of our country, would be shuddered at and passed as worse than a moral charnel house.

But what means should be used? The only effectual means were to employ men who might gain the confidence of that community, and become the repositories of the fearful crimes that had made Leoni notorious. Experience taught this truth—that crime stalks not in the sun light, but loves darkness. You will remember that while the obstructing of an engine is the most fearful and terrible crime that the human mind can contemplate, it is also one easily accomplished, with every protective against detection. It can be done in the night time, by a single arm and in a single moment. You will remember that the guilty bosom unburthens itsely only to what it deems a kindred spirit. You will remember that, although these outrages continued during the space of two years, although every ordinary means of detection was resorted to, no guilty perpetrator was detected. It was in vain that ordinary police were stationed along the road. The allies of this fearful combination were in every place—they penetrated into the offices of our prison agents—they insinuated themselves even into the employment of the company—they were apprised of every ordinary movement—and whenever a watch was placed the spot was known, and the offender passed further on; they laughed at every ordinary precaution, and grew fearfully bold from lengthened impunity. From the breaking of a hand car in '49, they made rapid strides, till in 1850 they contemplated the shooting of every engineer, the entombing of whole trains, and the burning of depots. And, gentlemen, you will not forget the significant fact, that although it is conceded that these outrages were continued for years, no offender was discovered till these spies were employed. Somebody did those deeds, for they were the work of human hands; butuntil spies were employed, no single act was ever traced to the conviction of its perpetrator.

But you are asked why did they not employ wholly men of high character and position, instead of the graduates of State Prison; a wise question truly. I fear gentlemen that even if the Company could have induced the loftiest and best of our citizens,such menfor instance as Bishop McCoskry or Dr. Duffield, who I see have honored us on this occasion with their presence, to undertake such an office, their exalted characters would have added little to the success of their undertakings. I fear that ere they could win the confidence of these defendants, they would have to serve a long tutelage under the Rev. Mr. Billings, the accomplished guide and preceptor of the unfortunate Hawley. I fear even my respected friend, General Williams. who sits before you, or any other man distinguished for high character and integrity would fare no better. It is idle to talk; the dictate of every rational mind is the best assurance that the class of men employed were of the right character and stamp.

But again, gentlemen mark the extra and abundant caution taken. Altho' the Company had faith in the truthfulness of these men, they resolved to satisfy the public also; they guarded against the possibility of false accusations; no statement from any source—subject even to suspicion was acted upon until abundantly corroborated. The evidence has shown you this; thus when Phelps reported the important fact that Gay had confessed the burning and exhibited a match, Messrs. Van Arman and Clark took pains to assure themselves of the truth of the report, that in due time they might assure you. When the Niles match was to be delivered "honest John Faulkner," as, even the prisoners counsel have called him,was sent for to be present,that no deception might be practiced. And so throughout all the evidence; altho' it has been again and again rung in your ears that this prosecution rested entirely on the evidence of Phelps, Lake and Wescott, you will find in fact, that every material thing which *they* prove,is also proved or corroborated by other witnesses against whom no breath of suspicion can be raised. You will remember that the learned counsel, tho' he might well trust to his own eloquence, pressed to his aid the eloquence of others, and cited a long passage from Addison on spies—the context would show you that Addison spoke of those who became spies for a culpable purpose. When the counsel took the trouble of transcribing the passage that he might read it to you from his manuscript, I regret that he omitted the following sentence which would have rendered the quotation strictly applicable: "As it is absolutely necessary for rulers to make use of other peoples eyes and ears, they should take particular care to do it in such a manner that it may not bear too hard on the person whose life and conversation are inquired into." You will perceive gentlemen that in this case the advice of Addison has been strictly followed.

Having thus disposed of matters which, though not strictly in the case, I could not suffer to pass unanswered, I will proceed to a calm investigation of the evidence. I will answer the points taken by counsel one by one, and as nearly as possible in the same order in which they were presented. As I take them up I will read the testimony bearing upon them. I will endeavor to point out the particulars in which I conceive that testimony has been misrepresented: And I ask you gentlemen to watch closely that I state the testimony fairly and truly--I respectfully request the court to correct me when I err, and shall be pleased and grateful if counsel for defendants will admonish me whenever I read the testimony unfairly or misstate any of their propositions. My sole desire is to ascertain the truth, and enable you to take a fair, just, impartial and comprehensive view of this case.

You will find as I proceed gentlemen, that I shall not weary you by any elaborate argument—for a statement of each point urged by the defence, and the reading of the testimony bearing upon it, will in most instances be a sufficient answer.

The learned counsel has gravely told you that Phelps was the first who ever mentioned the subject of burning—that to burn a depot and charge it upon his friends at the Centre was a proposition by Phelps to Gay, and having laid this unfounded basis, all thro' his address he continues the idea and argues that every scheme charged upon the defendants partakes of the character of this, *the* first design and hence must have originated in the same brain.

This argument falls to the ground if the design was the plan of Gay and not Phelps. Nay more,the argument would remain to prove by their similitude that the others also were the offspring of Gay and his associates—"his friends at the Centre."

To decide between myself and the counsel I refer you to the testimony of Phelps on page 9, where he relates his first interview with Gay.

"The conversation was first introduced by speaking of some men who had been arrested for counterfeiting--one Van Sickles and Van Houton, and what would be the best mode of getting Van Sickles liberated. *Gay proposed* several modes, and mentioned the burning of one of three or four of the depots of the Central Railroad,and stated the mode by which he could be liberated by the burning of a depot. The plot was as follows:

Mr. Van Sickles, who was then on bail, for counterfeiting, could be placed in jail—the depot at Ypsilanti, Ann Arbor, or some other one be burned, and on furnishing information of who fired it, Van Sickles could get released, and they could also doubtless get $1,000 reward from the Railroad Company, for the information, besides getting $200 from his (Gay's) *friends* for setting the fire.

It was suggested that the burning should be laid to Joseph Boyce."

Also to Mr. Clark's testimony, page 12.

Heard from Gay his plot of charging the burning of the depot upon Boyce, (as related by Mr. Phelps.)

Also, the testimony of Mr. Van Arman on page 12.

"Went to Gay's house again the next night, and had a conversation with him—Gay said they could get $1000 for burning the depot at Niles, and divulged his plot for swearing it upon Jo. Boyce, by a man and his wife."

I think I am safe then gentlemen, in asserting that according to the evidence,the plot was the suggestion of Gay,and *not* Phelps;and the design of Gay was to charge the burning on Boyce, and *not* upon "his friends at the Centre."

There is much force in the argument of counsel that a similarity of design indicates identity of authorship. We find Hawley testifying as follows in regard to Phelps:

"He told me he wanted me to burn a depot in Detroit, and that he would give me a sum, I think $50, for doing it; he said the R. R. Co. would offer a large reward, that he and I would swear it upon men who lived on the road and who had their cattle killed or were otherwise injured—that I should have my share of the reward."

Here is the Boyce plan slightly varied, and whence does it come; not from Phelps—he denied it, and Hawley has in your presence confessed that he swore falsely; that he was suborned to commit deliberate perjury; that he never saw Phelps; that the words I have read were put into his mouth by the Rev. Mr. Billings,the friend, pastor, partizan, and associate of these defendants. Gentlemen, further comment on this point is unnecessary.

The learned counsel also urged upon you the improbability of Gay confessing his crimes so freely while at the same time he asserted he would place himself in the power of no man. But you will remember gentlemen, altho' I perceive it is not so reported *in the published* testimony—that the remark of Gay was in answer to a questton by Mr. Van Arman whether when he saw the Prosecuting Attorney in relation to Boyce, he would inform him that he knew who burned the depot, and Gay replied, "he was'nt such a d——d fool as to place himself in any man's power."

If this is a true statement of the testimony,and counsel do not seem disposed to deny it, this point also is answered by reference to the evidence, for however natural it was that Gay should not place himself in the power of the public prosecution, it was equally natural that he should unbosom himself and boast of his offences to those whom he deemed equally abandoned and criminal with himself.

Mark me gentlemen, I do not charge these misrepresentations as the result of design, as the gentlemen had *only four months* to compile their extracts, they may be the result of haste; but I do charge that as we proved, we shall find that every point made by the defence is based upon similar accidental perversions of the testimony.

Another favorite theory with the defence is, that when first on the stand in May, Phelps did not name the persons whom Gay stated had procured the burning of the depot—that instead of the name he used the phraseology of "the persons." Truly, so he did, but why; because on that day the prosecution stipulated to introduce only evidence respecting Gay, and under it the defendant's counsel objected to the witnesses mentioning the name of any defendant save Gay, and therefore the expression of "the person I," was used.

The counsel for defendants has ingeniously argued that as there is no communication shown between Gay and these defendants, that therefore they were strangers and unknown to each other. Let the testimony speak.

Phelps tells you on his first examination that Gay informed him that he got the match from *his friends*; and, altho' neither Mr. Van Arman or Phelps were suffered on the first day to mention who those friends were, when Mr. Van Arman was recalled for cross examination the defence opened the door, and at page 174 he testifies in relation to the same interview with Gay:

"On the last night we were at Gay's he told us he burnt the Depot last fall, and that he was hired to do it by his friends at Michigan Centre; said they would give him $200 for burning the new depot which he said was $50 more than he got for burning the old one. He mentioned the names of Fitch, Filley, Mount, and I think O. D. Williams as among his friends; wished Clark and me to go immediately up to Michigan Centre with him and get acquainted with them. Said his friends at the Centre, had furnished him with the tools to burn the depot. He wanted us to come up next day, and spoke of the plan to burn and lay it to Boyce; said he would see Stuart the next day and see whether Boyce was in jail."

Lake also,at page 164 tells us that Mount said "he knew Gay since he was a child, and had come to this country with him." Does not this testimony answer the objection? will it be said that Gay only pretended to know these defendants when we find him urging Clark and Van Arman to accompany him immediately to the Centre to be introduced to them? Will it be said that his connection with them was of an innocent character when the very business on which he wished to introduce supposed criminals, was connected with breaking jails, burning depots, and passing counterfeit money? The impress of truth is on the narration, it comes to you from the lips of two gentlemen of character and reputation; it shows that Gay for once at least was truthful; that he was since in the confession he made; and that he was linked by no common ties with the men to whom he felt such assurance in intruding with two supposed malefactors. And yet, you are told there is nothing to show that Gay knew any of these defendants. But you were told so not in connection with the whole, but a selection of the testimony. It is not necessary to refer to the testimony of Phelps in reference to the interviews between Fitch and Gay in February, nor that of Wescott in relation to the night visit of Fitch to Gay's house, to show association; the testimony of Clark and Van Arman alone establishes an intimacy of no common character between them.

You are, however, told to be cautious lest you sacrifice the rights of citizens to the *behests* of dangerous monopolies. If the warning was heeded, it might be well enough if conveyed in the spirit of moderation, but when coming with malignant fierceness, it was not difficult to perceive that the "energetic bile" of the eminent counsel was *permitted* to gush forth for none other than sinister purposes.

Gentlemen, I respectfully submit that in this country we have little to fear from the power—the "undue influence," or the "bloated wealth" of corporations. It is not with them, or us, here as in the old world. Here, public opinion, public prejudice, and watchful jealousy are so powerful, so wide spread and so vigilant, that no incorporated body would long venture to trifle with, or unnecessarily dare them. The

2*

law is so easy of access, its administration so public, and so subject to review, and the spirit of the age so distrustful of aggregated power, that redress, so open to every citizen, is sure to protect him against undue encroachments, and, in truth, gives him the vantage ground over his apparently stronger antagonist. Again, the stock of these incorporated bodies are owned by large portions of the people themselves, from various parts of the country; are controlled by divers views, and represented by different spirits; are constantly changing hands, by sales and by death, and consequent devise and inheritance; but over and above all, such bodies as the M. C. Railroad Company are essentially dependant on and identified with the good will of the people, and the increase, prosperity, and welfare of the country, and in fact, possess few, if any of the objectionable features of "hated monopolies." They are absolutely necessary. Individual effort would never accomplish their great ends, and without them this expansive country of ours, now bound together by iron bonds, with its every wealth and power developing, with its most distant points brought near together, and with its broad surface all over lustrous with glowing prosperity, would have dragged and halted in her bright career. The advance of weeks now, would have required years; distancc would still separate friends and interrupt business. The wide extent of our country, instead of being a blessing, might have proved a curse and cause of separation, for far distance and long absence, great inconveniencs and apparent contrary and distinct interests, would soon chill old associations, and turn the current and spirit of portions of the county to other projects and different views.

I submit that the history of such Corporations, their past doings, present deeds, and future prospects, in this country, should not lead us to too much distrust. They have done well for the whole country, and promise still brighter and broader visions and fruitions for us and for our children.

Take New England for an example of the fruits of "hated monopolies." With an uninviting soil, a eold climate, a rugged and rock strewed land; what has corporation and joint capital done for her?—What has it not done! It struck the rock and the living waters of her power, gushed forth; it has trammeled her mountains; dammed her rivers, crowned her with Manufactories; made her days and nights tremulous with the power of her machinery; given labor to the people; dotted her over with churches, colleges and school-houses; covered and clustered her with art, and science, and wealth, and knowledge; with peace and refinement, power and glory, until her sons in every clime and land, burst forth with proud exclamations at the thought and name of their own New England. And all this can be done for our wider, broader, and more glorious West—if undue distrust, jealousy and preference, are not unnecessarily and wickedly spread among our people.

Gentlemen, I cannot but express my regret at the poisoned and dangerous sentiments which have been uttered in deliberate argument before you. I regret them the more, that they come from so distinguished a source; that they are not the fevered utterance of heated debate, but the studied embodiment of careful thought.

Doubtless the speech of the eminent Counsel is to go far and wide through the land, and to attract the admiration of at least his peculiar followers. I take it for granted—I sincerely hope, that, ere it ushers forth in print, it will be stripped of some of its destructive spirit and doctrine.

What! are we, in this law-abiding and loyal State, to have it thundered in the ears of jurors, in the sanctity of a court-house, and in the course of judicial proceedings, from the lips of any man, that if a verdict is not satisfactory to the people, another "inquisition will be holdén, and the victims of the law be dragged from the bloody fingers of power?" Do I overstate it? No—I know you recollect it. I saw and felt, and sympathized with you, in the shudder which marked your feelings as that and kindred sentences fell upon your astonished ears. I forgot I was here, and was carried for a moment to some heated tribune of Paris, where some spirit of fierceness was maddening the populace and stirring up France to again

"Get drunk with blood to vomit crime "

Ah! gentlemen, there is a worse evil abroad through this land, than the overshadowing power of Corporations. There are *isms* of dreadful and fearful import around us. They "menace our public institutions and private rights." There is a spirit of disloyalty to law and country; a tendency to forsake the old landmarks; to treat the lessons of sages which come down from our fathers, as antiquated and worn-out; to speak lightly of our hallowed Union; to abandon those pure, steadfast, and perpetual principles which have sanctified our past, and which can alone save our future; and to rear and plant in *their* stead a "*higher law*," which, each one for himself, may adjudge and administer.

Hence come, those frightful dangers which disturb our courts; that voice of evil omen which would fain chaunt the hymn of ruin over the broken fragments of our capitol; which would raise the arm of private judgment against the enactments of the law-makers; and rouse an excited populace to sit in judgment on the decisions of courts and the verdicts of juries.

Gentlemen, it is an evil day, when the men of our high places are found scattering such seed in congenial soil. Where, if such is to be the course of things, are we to stop? There would be an end of law, and confusion and ruin would stalk with fearful strides over our land. We enforce not the law here by the bayonet. It is the law of the people, administered by forms prescribed; and the beautiful sight is exhibited of the people of a whole empire bowing in silent respect and cheerful obedience to the adjudications of their own courts and the verdicts of their own juries. And well may we do so. For what would we be without that law and cheerful obedience to it? What and where would we be if a community, or any portion of it, could or dare rise up, in violence or lawlessness, and crush or disturb the solemn awards of legal tribunals? What and how shall we characterize the spirit which would invite us to such a dread feast?

Gentlemen, all you possess on earth, is the reward of laborprotected by law. It is law alone which keeps all things in order—guards the sleep of infancy, the energy of manhood, and the weakness of age. It hovers over us by day; it keeps watch and ward over the slumbers of the night; it goes with us over the land, and guides and guards us through the trackless paths of the mighty waters. The high and the low, each are within its view, and beneath its ample folds. It protects beauty and virtue, punishes crime and wickedness, and vindicates right. Honor and life, and liberty and property, the wide world over, are its high objects. Stern, yet kind—pure, yet pitying—steadfast, immutable and just; it is the attribute of God on earth. It proceeds from his bosom, and encircles the world with its care and power and blessings. All honor and praise to those who administer it in purity, and who reverence its high behests.

When our own respected, eloquent, and classic citizen Senator, was desired to choose a motto and design for the coat of arms of that State, with which he is so identified, and by it so appreciated, most happy was he in that choice. We find it stamped, and reading, when rendered, thus: "If you seek a beautiful peninsula, look around you." And we see, as part of the design, the sun of civilization rising from the waters, and commerce and agriculture quickening into life beneath its genial rays. And the lone Indian is there too, standing in sadness, seeing the elements advancing and gathering which tell him the doom of his race, and before which he must again retreat to roam the western wilds.

And a beautiful peninsula it is! Its shores bathed and almost circled by the majestic lakes which now are convulsed with storm, and anon flash back the serene light of heaven, as if from a million of mirrors. Its prairies blooming with beauty, and uttering sweet whisperings to the light wind as it breathes among its flowers. Its fields yellow with luxuriant harvests. Its youth cultivated. Its people moral, contented and happy. And all reposing beneath the reign of law and order. But change the scene! Let law be disregarded, and her ministers brought to contempt—let confusion and disobedience characterize her people, and the clouds of darkness and disgrace will soon gather over our land. Frantic passion will produce ruthless violence; bad men will revel and rejoice; the good will sigh and depart. Better, than that this should come to pass, would it be that the forest and primeval silence should return again. But it is useless to anticipate such evil things. Such invocations to our people, fall on unwelcoming ears. They may suit some foreign district, some land where anti-rent and anti-law make part of her history; but cannot and will not corrupt the law-loving and law-respecting people of Michigan. He who expects to read on the columns of her greatness, words of disloyalty to the Union or disrespect to law, may seek for them in vain, until he himself sinks into the abyss of time.

I regret, gentlemen, to have thus to leave the strict merits of the case, to follow and comment on the extraneous, and to my judgment most dangerous, remarks of counsel; and will now return to what is more in point.

We are told, gentlemen, that this is not an indictment for conspiracy. There was little need to argue that point, as the prosecution have never asserted or pretended it was. The indictment is for arson; and the defendants now on trial are charged as accessories before the fact. The charge is simply this: that Gay burned the depot, and these defendants induced and procured him to do it. But, although not an indictment for conspiracy, it is for a crime resulting from conspiracy among the defendants; and wherever combination exists, the law relating to conspiracy is applicable, although the charge is not one of mere conspiracy. It has been so held in many cases. But I will trespass on your time only by reading one. [Here counsel read and commented on the case, The Commonwealth *vs.* Crowninshield, 10 Pick. 497.]

And, gentlemen, notwithstanding all the arguments and assertions of counsel, it is the law, that wherever combination exists, it is competent to give in evidence, not only the acts done, but also the words spoken by those who belong to the conspiracy, and which are within the scope of the combination.

In the case of the Queen *vs.* Murphey, 34 English C. L. R. p. 600, Justice Coleridge uses the following language:

"There are two general observations which I ought to make. The first observation is, that from the nature of this charge the evidence must necessarily grow up as the case proceeds. The acts of the one party must be given in evidence, and then the acts of the other, and it may then be shown that those acts fully prove a conspiracy between them. The other observation is, that my brother Bompas (quere Gov. Seward,) confounds *what is evidence to be heard*, with what is evidence to convict. It has been opened that these two defendants instigated a general resistance to the church-rates and that they published handbills on the 26th and 27th of October, and this was on the evening of the 27th; these handbills too were calculated to cause that which took place and added to this we find that when the party is brought before the Magistrate one of the defendants *assisted him in his defence* and *the other became his bail*. I cannot say that there is no evidence, that this act was instigated by the defendants."

Such acts and declarations being in evidence you are bound to consider them. You may deem them insufficient to convict on, but you cannot disgard them, you must allow them such weight as your best judgment dictates. And so we respectfully ask the court to charge you.

In this case the obstructions and other acts of aggression committed in Leoni, when taken in connection with the language used on all occasions by defendants, must have no slight influence on your minds; they must go *far* to point out these defendants as the nistigators of the particular crime charged in the indictment.

Let me give you an illustration. If these persons stood charged with the burning of this building; if it was proven that they had repeatedly threatened to destroy the property of its owner; that they had combined together to do him all the injury in their power; to assault him; to destroy his business; to steal his property, and failing in that, to burn his house, and the building is thereafter in fact fired, will not a suspicion amounting almost to the certainty of guilt fasten upon those who have thus threatened and conspired? will not the mind inquire who so likely to do it?

And how much stronger is the case before you where we find these defendants constantly assembling; breathing forth vengeance against this company; threatening to destroy its property; to obstruct its engines; to murder not only its employees but even unknown and innocent travellers who dare to patronize it; and as a last resort to *burn its depots*. When we find them for the space of two years, constantly acting under the spur of their diabolical hatred, and as I shall hereafter show you with community of action and design, carrying their vile threats into execution.

You will readily perceive gentlemen, how important it was to the prosecution to prove the obstructions and other acts of aggression committed by these defendants, in and about Leoni, and that they were the result of a combination between them. The defence has felt the weight and importance of this proof, and a strenuous effort has been made to convince you that there is no proof of a combination. It seems conceded in argument that some of these defendants committed some of these acts, but the counsel says each act was done on the impulse of the moment: was the individual act of the person doing it, and there was no concert, no agreement, no combination.

Now the prosecution contends that these acts were done by the defendants under a general combination and understanding amongst them to injure this road in every way, and to the greatest extent in their power.

This is an important branch of this case, and before entering on a detail of the evidence, I beg to read to you a few authorities showing how combination may be proved.

Starkie on evidence, vol. 2 No. 232 & 233, says:

"A convict may be proved by evidence of a concurrence of the acts of the defendant with those of the others convicted together by a correspondence in point of them, and in their manifest adaptation to effect the same object; such evidence is moee or less strong according to the average publicity or privacy of the object of concurrence; and according to the greater or less degree of similarity in the means and measures adopted by the parties, the more secret the one and the greater the coincidence in the other, the stronger is the evidence of the conspiracy."

"Where several combine together for the same illegal purpose each is the agent of all the rest, and any act done by one in furtherence of the unlawful design, is, in consideration of law the act of all. Thus you perceive, gentlemen, that if we find a similarity of action and a similarity of expressed motive in the purpetrators of these outrages; if we find that each act tended to accomplish the same object, that all, or nearly all these defendants were identified with these acts of aggression; that they were conversed of freely amongst them, and that the perpetrators of each act sought the first occasion to communicate their exploit to the rest of the defendants;

the first of combinatien will be established beyond all dispute, to the full extent of all that can be embraced within its scope.

In citing testimony, I will refer to the printed report and I invite you and the counsel to follow me and at once correct me if I color or misrepresent it. I will also point out as I pass along, where and how the evidence has been misrepresented or suppressed by the learned counsel on the other side.

The counsel who preceded me, mentioned eleven assaults and menaces against the road, claiming that with not one of them was even one single defendant identified; and seventeen overt acts with none of which, he claimed, was any defendant identified, save Filley, Williams, and the two Prices. I will take up these twenty eight assaults and overt acts in the same order in which they were presented by him, and see if the testimony he has read, that which *he has not read*, will not lead us to a very different result; and then I will add to the list some ten or a dozen acts of aggression which *in his hurry* he omitted. He also claimed that even in the few instances where Filley, Williams and the Prices were identified, the acts resulted from impulse, were individual; and that there was no evidence of concort or combination.

1. The cars were stoned. Proved by Holmes, none of the defendants identified.

2. In June '49 the cars were stoned—one stone fell near a lady, another struck a gentleman on the breast and hurt him severely. Proved by Levi Easter.

3. Stones on another occasion were thrown by eight or ten persone from some bushes, at the cars. Proved by Caster.

The prosecution concedes that there is no evidence to directly identify any of the defendants with either these three acts, but here I must myke my first complaint against the candor of counsel inasmuch as he has altogether omitted the following important portion of Carters testimony found on page 76: "Have several times been obliged to stop and remove obstructions in that vicinity during the past two years; was baggage man on passenger train in '48. For a long time were obliged to run a hand car ahead of the passenger train, and have three times got off in one night to remove obstructions, such as rails, old ties, strap iron, &c; the passenger train had to run very slow; this was between Grass Lake and Jackson; during '49 have known the track to be obstructed as often as a dozen times." This is certainly proof of other obstructions no where named in the counsels list.

Wescott speaking of Fitch at page 80, says:

"In march 1850, he told me what had been done in '49; said the boys placed obstructions on the track; the way they did it was by being secreted in the timbered land between the Centre and Jackson; after the hand car passed they would rush out and place things on the track, before the passenger train come up; also said they would place pieces of strap iron between the joints of the T. rail and cover them with bushes and branches of catnip."

Charles Rogers, at pages 116 & 117, says of Filley: "I worked for Filley and Fitch in harvest '49; near Filley's house on the road heard him speak of throwing the cars off; it was in fall of '49; they were running a hand car ahead of the train; said a stick of timber could be placed on the culvert so as to lean off the track while the hand car passed, but by means of a rope attached to the lower end, a person at a distance could pull it so as to bring the timber in connection with the train."

and of Fitch he says:

"Heard him speaking of a grand invention for throwing the cars off; either said there had been or might be a machine by which the cars could be thrown off, and the machine saved for another time: said in the noise and confusion of the cars being thrown off, the machine could be taken away."

I think gentlemen, the testimony of these four witnesses, shows conclusively, that, in '49, the cars were frequently obstructed, and that Fitch and Filley, if not others of defendants, were either the actual aggressors or the instigators—not acting from impulse either, but deliberately devising subtle means to frustrate the protection afforded by running hand cars. From Rogers we learn they *devised* the means. From Carter that their object *was accomplished*; and from Wescott, that Fitch confessed his participations.

4. The cars were stoned. John H. Dexter at page 100 says:

"The night previous to the suit, the cars were stoned. I had just gone to bed and heard the glass jingle; went down and told Filley somebody had thrown glass into the parlor window; he said he guessed not; went and looked but found no glass broken; it was while the cars were passing; found Fitch, Filley and two or three others out of doors. The Price boys were about before I went to bed. I afterwards saw glass on the railroad track, six or eight rods from where they stood; afterwards, saw two piles of stones in Filley's orchard, about the right size to throw."

So much of the testimony, the counsel read and claimed: no defendant was implicated; he overlooked the following evidence of H. C. Dexter, on page 106.

"I was at Filley's the night the cars were stoned. I was standing near and heard a stone hit the cars; Price, Corwin, Eitch and Filley were there; saw Filley have a bottle in his hand, and swinging it as the cars passed, at the time the glass windows in the cars jingled from stones thrown. It was a passenger train going west."

This last testimony was too much for the counsel; he was afraid of *the bottle* and wisely omitted it, but now that you have it, gentlemen, how will you avoid the conclusion, that Filley, who swung the bottle and those who stood beside him and who, in other portions of the testimony are found threatening to do such deeds, were the perpetrators of this *overt* act. You perceive gentlemen, how important it is to have the *entire* testimony as to each act.

5. Three stonings of the cars which are afterwards mentioned in the testimony of Woliver—proved by Clark. Here also, the counsel omitted to state that Wm. Clark proved he met many obstructions in '49, generally between Fitch's and Filley's—that they had to run

hand cars there, but always thonght themselves safe *when they passed Leoni*, and so it is through the entire case: witness after witness fixes the conviction in our minds that every act of aggression originated amid the peaceful hamlets of Leoni.

6. Menaces by unknown persons, proved by Cochran and Sherman—tis true these men are not identified, but they come from Filley's—however, we do not claim there is any identification, so I pass to No.

7. Five shots fired at the engine house, proved by Clark. I pass this for the present, but will, when I reach No. 27, show you that many of the defendants are identified with it.

8. A slight obstruction which was carried off by the broom. With this we claim no identification.

9. Wescott, at page 88, says:

"I heard Fitch say when a mail car was burnt up, that the Co. lost $12,000, and a woman lost $4,000; Filley said the Co. after getting a few more such slaps would begin to think *there was a God in Israel*."

There is something in the form of expression used that indicates knowledge, but I have a long list to go through, and will concede that, even in this case, there is no proof against defendants.

10. Caswell proves a hand car was broken and that Filley said "the man who broke it knew who did it, he probably lives nearest to it." You will remember that *it is* in proof that Filley lived *nearest*, and had before threatened that the hand car should be broken every night. Evidence, gentlemen, which comes very close upon direct proof, though we do not claim any identified with it, save Filley.

11. Smith and Marsh prove the placing of a piece of flat iron on the track by defendant Tyrrell. We concede there is no direct proof implicating any other defendant with this act, but I must dissent from the proposition that this was a harmless act, that could work no injury. If the learned counsel lived in our state, and was in the habit of riding over the road, he would be far from regarding the placing of pieces of iron on the track as an *innocent* amusement.

12. Knox and Van Valen proved some acts of Doctor Farnham's near Marshall; there can be no doubt of the truthfulness of these witnesses, but the acts seem so foolish that there is fair reason to question if the witnesses may not have been mistaken as to the real character of the transaction.

13. The testimony relating to this overt act was thus given to you by the learned counsel from *his abstract*:

"The prosecution dwell upon the burning of a culvert, east of Filley's house, in June, '51, proved by W. B. Stanton. He says that he was at Filley's, "that Mrs. Filley came in and gave the alarm that the culvert was on fire. Stanton and Fitch went up to see it. Stanton proposed to get water and put out the fire. Fitch, with his usual smile. (for he was always pleasant to me,) answered, 'you will have to go out of this town to find anybody to put it out.' "

I must ask you to compare this with the true testimony on page 99.

True, there is not much difference in *words*, but it is an apt illustration of the use the learned counsel can make of a smile *properly placed.* The counsel passes this point lightly; the testimony seems scarce worth his notice. It was but a smiling allusion, by Fitch, to the tone of public feeling. Do you think so, gentlemen? How came Mr. Fitch to be so well assured of the sentiments of his neighbors, these defendants? One of the most essential ingredients of combination is mutual understanding, and we find it fully developed here. Fitch can speak, not only for himself, but for all Leoni. This was no trivial affair. Even though Fitch's lips were wreathed with his "usual smile," this was no smiling matter. It was a daring outrage, and were it not for the warning given to Spaulding by Stanton, it would have been a fearful and calamitous one. Yet, knowing that the train was rushing on with hot speed, and hundreds of unsuspecting passengers—knowing that if it came unwarned a fearful destruction of property and life must ensue, Mr. Fitch not only would not help himself, but he could smilingly speak with certainty for his friends and neighbors that they too would decline. How far removed from a murderer is the man who, by the lifting of his arm, can save the lives of hundreds, yet "looks calmly on, smiles and sees them perish!" Here the counsel, who last addressed you, took occasion, *en passant*, to quietly state that it was very clear that Phelps and Lake made this burning the basis of a perjury, but are detected, as by mistake they fix the burning in February, '51, when it occurred in June '50. The *argument* is perfect, but *the facts* are *assumed.* There were two culverts burned. Phelps and Lake spoke of a culvert burned in '51, Stanton of one burned in '49, and there is not a particle of proof to indicate that they meant to refer to the same transaction.

14. The testimony of the two Dexters who prove a wood pile was burned near the Centre,that shortly before the alarm they heard a person come in barefooted and pass stealthily towards Filley's room; that Filley would not go to the fire as he feared spies would see him; and of Hudson who found two foot prints near the fire, one of which he thinks was Filley's, and who says that when he accused Filley of the deed, instead of denying it he replied, "there should be no fence built till they settled for his lands"—bring this act so home, that counsel concedes Filly may have done it, but claims it was his own solitary act. He forgets, I believe he did not state to you, that Hudson found the foot prints of two persons—so that it was not the act of Filley alone—he had some accomplice.

15 Woliver proves that he and Corwin took a spindle from Fitch's and placed it in the frog to run off the train, and that the next morning Fitch said, "you must not take anything from my house or they will suspect me. Take anything else you can find, but nothing from my house." Counsel claims that no person was identified with this but Corwin ; that Fitch had no part in it, no knowledge of it, till after it was done. You will not fail to ask if Fitch's language was that of encouragement or reproof? and whether the immediate information possessed by Fitch does not evidence a general understanding to commit and encourage depredations?

16 Clark proves that in October 1850,the engine Rocket was thrown

off. Sherman proved that in speaking of it, Corwin said, " *we* did it." Yet counsel claims this was the sole act of Corwin; it is true there is no explanation given of who was meant by " we," but it meant some persons. Corwin had some accomplices—who were they? Who were his constant associates? Who day after day joined him in threats against this road and pledged themselves to *like* unholy deeds? The counsel overlooked the testimony of Purcill on pages 123 and 4: "I was at the Centre when the locomotive Rocket was run off last of August or 1st of September, about 9 P. M.; saw Corwin there with two others; twenty or twenty five minutes before the train came along; Corwin said they had been to a husking bee; but did not think he should go again in the open field; it was a pretty cold night; they asked Filley to treat, which he did; a short time after Grant came in and said the passenger train had run off on the east switch. Holden, who was with me, said let's go to the train and they commenced talking privately together; this was in Filley's bar-room; they were talking privately when Grant came in. In reply to Holden, they said they would be along soon; but they did not come; we went back and found them at Filley's." It is conceded Corwin did it, and we find him and his accomplices rushing straight from their work to Filley's to be treated and to have a private talk. There is no crime in treating, no crime in speaking privately; but can you, in the face of this testimony, come to any conclusion but that Corwin and the others did the deed, and that Filley was privy to it? Why did not these men go down to the engine with Holden and Stanton? If innocent, was it not natural they should do so? Gentlemen, the murderer shrinks from the presence of his cold and lifeless victim, and these men, not yet informed of the consequences of their fearful deed, might well turn from the spot that, for ought they knew, was steeped with blood, that cried out to heaven for vengeance against them.

17. An attempt to detach freight trains, and stone the conductors, proved by Carter and Sherman. Corwin is the only defendant who made the attempt, but by referring to the testimony of Woliver, on page 55, you will find that other outrages was contemplated, that night, and were abandoned because of the presence of two strangers at the tavern, supposed to be *spies*, that a number of defendants were round the tavern, that night and that Filley and Champlin in particular were active in learning whether these strangers were spies,—a clear indication that they at least were privy to the intended operations—else why should they interest themselves as to the spies? If they were privy to any baffled design they are accountable for any substituted one, having the same object.

18. Woliver proves that in September '50 he and Filley turned a rail near the dry marsh. The learned counsel read you the testimony of Woliver, and no more and complacently assured you that there was no evidence of concert—like all the rest it was an individual unpremeditated act—no concert—no privity with others. I will read some other portions of testimony to you. By referring to the testimony of Brown, page 79 and 80—you will find that he saw con-

cealed under Filley's barn, tools for tearing up the track: that Filley once told him he had such tools—and that subsequently he found the same, or exactly similar ones, concealed under Filley's fence near the marsh (the place where this outrage was committed.) On page 55, you will find that when Corwin wanted Sherman to turn a switch, he said, "he would go and see Filley and find where the *iron bars* were for the operation." And at page 57 you find E. Price saying "he had made a couple of *bars* to take up the track." Yet the eminent counsel tells you there is no proof of concert—no common design. Truly gentlemen, if the most important portion of the testimony is to be suppressed, we may seek in vain for evidence of combination, but read the entire—read it fairly; and you find "*combination*" stamped on every page. Is there not combination and preconcert here? Price made the tools—Filley had possession of them; but they were common property; when Corwin or any other accomplice needed them, he had but to ask and they were given. But each act you are told, is the result of the impulse of the moment. Tools are prepared—plans are laid months before hand, that all may be ready when a favorable moment presents itself; and because the hour, and day, and moment of opportunity cannot be foretold, but are promptly seized on when they come, there is no forethought, no preconcert. No concert—when we find men doing the same deeds—using the same tools, breathing the same threats, and aiming at the same end! I have read you the law on this point and you will not be imposed on by sophistry.

19. The counsel tells you, Woliver proves he and Filley placed a tie in the culvert, so it broke the lamp; that Fitch speaking of it next day, said he had gone up and while the engineers were engaged revised the breaks, and that it otherwise appears Fitch got home about the time the accident happened; and as usual says this was the sole act of Filley—no one else privy.

Allow me gent'emen to read you the *balance* of the testimony on this point, not read by counsel; there are more privies than the counsel mentioned, and the proof does not rest on Woliver alone, though I will show you hereafter that he is worthy of trust and credit. Dixson page 72 says:

"Heard Fitch say he went up to where the cars stopped; think he said he and Lemn went up, but am not positive; he said Lemn had said he took a large jack-knife with him, and slipped it up into his coat sleeve, as he did not know but he might have occasion to use it; the obstruction was old ties."

At page 82 Wescott says of Fitch:

"He said they had a 'fuss, the night before, near his house; an engine was obstructed, and said they laid it to me, and said 'd—n 'em, they laid it to me, but I told them I did not get home;' we walked up to the spot, and he explained how the timbers were placed, to break the lamp, which he said must have cost $100. Before I saw Fitch, Hay told me of the accident; heard that Lemn came home with Filley, and staid with him." "Williams has also told me that Fitch put on the brakes, and laughed at it as a joke."

Wells at page 60 says: "Another time heard Fitch, Filley and Eb. Price talk of a plan to place a rail in the track to strike the lamp; a few days afterwards heard Fitch say such a thing had happened toward Leoni; this was after he suggested the plan."

John H. Dexter page 100 says: "Heard Corwin, Fitch and Filley speak of obstructions on the track west of Fitch's; they said it was a pity the engine did not run off and smash the whole train. One of them, I forget which, said the stick was pointed, and placed so as to break the lamp."

Yet you are told with very assumption of candor, that this was the sole act of Filley,—there was no forethought—no concert—yet we find no less than five of the defendants privy to it, and three of them devising the *modus operandi,* long before-hand. How chanced it that all this important testimony was omitted by the counsel who assumed to give the entire?

20, 21, 22 and 23. Are the four cases of stoneing the cars testified to by Woliver. He states the first was was done by himself, Price, Champlin and Davis; the 2d and 3d by himself, two Prices and Corwin; and the last by himself, Filley, Corwin and Williams. The testimony on this point was fairly enough presented, save that counsel omitted to state that Sutton on page 108, heard Barrett speak with Woliver about the cars being stoned by him Woliver. But the counsel with a solemn countenance, claimed that there was no evidence of concert—that each act was the individual act of those doing it. How absurd—whenever these men meet on business or pleasure, whenever opportunity offers, they stone the cars; they are always ready—no inducement is necessary; all of them who chance to be present join in the act—yet because they do not meet, resolve, seperate, and agree to meet again before doing it, there is no concert!

24. The engine Goliah was thrown off the track at Leoni. Sherman proves Corwin said "they did it;" and Bingham page 108 proves that he that night was passed by Corwin and Williams in a buggy, speaking of the cars and fearing that "would be too late;" they were going towards where the accident happened, and before it happened that he recognized their voices, that Corwin spoke in a *feigned* voice. There can be no doubt from this testimony, but that Williams was one of the persons comprised in those mentioned by Corwin to Sherman.

25. A wood pile was burned near the Centre. The testimony as to this act has been fairly stated to you. It is briefly this:—you will find it on page thirty—On the way from Jackson, Corwin proposed to burn the wood; when they got to the Centre Price agreed to go with them; they stopped at Filley's; they said they were going fishing; Filley gave them an axe; Price said he hadn't the first d——d thing to fight with in case of trouble; Filley gave him a knife; wished them luck, and told them where they could get whiskey on their return. Although Corwin, Price and Woliver were the ones who burned the wood, from this testimony, gentlemen, you can have little doubt in concluding that Filley was cognizant of their designs. He knew they anticipated a fight and trouble. Neither can you

have much trouble in disposing of the sophistry which termed it an impulsive act: for Corwin meditated on it all the way from Jackson; and Price, unless his mind was already prepared, would not so readily have entered on a deed that, in case of detection, would expose him to fearful punishment.

26. The Gazelle was thrown off. Woliver proves that it was done by himself, Filley and the two Prices. This overt act was the subject of a long discussion; the counsel contended that only three of defendants are in any way identified. As the prosecution are of a very different opinion, and regard the testimony bearing on it as pregnant with evidence of combination, I must refer you again, and fully to it.

The witness Taylor proves he found under the culvert, when the accident occured, a paper produced in the following words:

"Michigan Centre, Aug. 19, 1850.

Mr. Price,—Sir:—I want you to be at the mild stake, this side Leoni, on Monday night, at about half past 9 o'clock. We intend to run the cars somewheare's about there; be sure and be there at the time.

By order of the Committee, W. CHAMPLAIN."

The learned counsel has told you, this was read upon the witness Holmes expressing an opinion that it was in Champlin's hand, but that on being recalled, Holmes retracted that opinion — said he thought it was not the writing of Champlin, but thought it more resembled the hand writing of Taylor. I read to you, gentlemen, from the re-examination of Holmes, and you will see whether he does retract his first opinion:

"The W. is not in the form generally made by Champlin: also I have never seen his signature other than Wm. W. Champlin: also he generally spells his name Cham-*plin*, and the signature to this letter is Cham-*plain*. I have an account in my possession in the hand writing of Mr. Taylor. Saw Taylor once write in a book: think I know his writing, and that it has more marks of his hand than of Champlin's.

Cross-ex'd. I spoke of this matter with Frink at the R. R. hotel. Was brought in to be a witness by defendants. Also spoke with Champlin himself, and he said it was not his hand writing; this was about two weeks ago. May have talked with Higby about it, think I did: at Michigan Centre learned he did not make his signature in that way, by seeing some of his writing: he also told me since I was sworn that he did not spell his name in that way: the old man also showed me his copy book where it is spelled different. Still think the form of the letters are the same as his hand writing, and still it would strike me as his hand. Never saw Taylor write but once; then he wrote a number of names of those who were boarding with me. Don't say it is Taylor's hand; the W. is formed like Taylor's, but the other letters are not."

Thss, gentlemen, is called retracting his evidence, and it is with a vengeance. It amounts simply to this, after undergoing a severe tutelage with professors Frink, Higby, and Champlin, the witness persuaded himself that the "W" differed some from the usual "W" of Champlin; but all the tutelage cannot prevent him still saying, "it would still strike me as his hand." "Don't say it is Taylor's hand." Tolerable strong proof, gentlemen, from a tutored and unwilling witness.

I will not refer to the other witnesses on this point, as the counsel himself seemed to value their evidence as little worth. Wescott you will remember, proves that Fitch, speaking of thisa ct, said, "the Gazelle got dry and ran down to the marsh for a drink." Act. page 83 and 84. Wescott further says:

"A. M. Sackrider brought up a load, nearly all strangers to me; that day heard conversation between Williams and Filley; W. asked F. for money, and F. replied, "I thought that this Gazelle matter was all settled;" W. replied he thought there was something due him yet; Filley said to him, Fitch had paid him $10, and he (Filley) had paid him $12, and wanted to know how much more he claimed in the Gazelle matter. W. said he would leave it to Filley, and F. asked him if $3 would be enough; he said he supposed it would; at this time Sackrider called them in to get drink, they were in the yard and I was around the corner of the house six or eight feet from them when I heard the conversation; I went into the bar-room then and sat down; they came in, and Filley asked me to chance a five dollar bill, which I did, and he gave Williams three dollars.

Mr. Sackrider, on page 99, says:

"I saw Filley hand Williams a bill which he told him was a three dollar bill; just before that I saw them out doors talking; at the same time I saw Wescott standing very still around the corner, about six feet from them; I called Filley in for something to drink; said he would be in soon, Wescott came in and set down; about five minutes after I called Filley again, and he and Williams came in; Filley asked me to change a five dollar bill; I told him I was "dead broke;" he then asked Wescott, and he changed the bill for him, and Filley handed Williams $3, and asked him if that would make it straight."

Wells also testifies to the payment of the $3. Stronger corroboration could not well be conceived. And how is it sought to be got rid of? Not by the testimony of Crowell who gave such an improbable version of the occurrence, the counsel wisely abstained from all allusion to him—although there was no doubt that the $3 was the amount paid, Crowell forgot the figure, and while he heard the accounts settled, and the items borrowed money, &c., specified, he was sure the ballance to be paid was $2. But the counsel says the prosecution witnesses all disagree. I deem that these very differences inherent evidence of truth. I will read them to you. Phelps, at page 128, narrating a conversation between himself, Williams, Price, Freeland, and Corwin, says:

"Williams—said you know I was the means of throwing off the cars west of Leoni, though I was at home and abed, and we can lay it on to Laycock and swear it on to him."

You will remember that this was not addressed to Phelps, but to others who were fully familiar with the entire occurrence. To them it would be quite intelligible, though to others involved and obscure. When Lake testifies, he says, at page 161.

"Williams said Corwin, Filley, Woliver, and two Prices were down there; and he furnished them with a bar to go and tear up the track, and he went home and went to bed, so he could be a witness for them if necessary, and swear that they were all at his house."

Here you will remember that Williams was explaining to Lake, who till then was ignorant. How natural the variation! How like truth! A hint did for the others, but to merely say he "was abed" would explain little to a stranger; he had to tell why he was abed.

The learned counsel omitted the testimony of Mr. Henry, who says, p. 98. "Heard Williams speak of the switch being turned, but said they could not lay it to him as he was abed." Why should Williams expect they would lay it to him? Gentlemen, "a guilty conscience needs no accuser;" and how ready the defence of this self accused sprung to his lip—he was abed. He had laid his plans, he was prepared for them there; he knew he could prove it. But the counsel says the witnesses implicate *different* def'ts. What of that? We do not assume that any one witness knows all—different portions come from different sources, and so coming and agreeing, they are the more entitled to credence. If, as the defence assumes, this was a got up story, the witnesses would agree in every material point; they would implicate the same men; their not doing so is evidence of the absence of collusion and helps to establish, what we firmly believe, that almost every def't was cognizant of and implicated in every aggression.

27. This, the last act referred to by the eminent counsel, relates to Fitch giving pistols to Wells, Laycock and Casswell, to shoot at the engine house. I will not follow the learned gentleman through the ingenious sophistry by which he sought to get rid of this fatal piece of testimony.

Here, as in other instances, you will find that there is in the pages in your hands, strong, direct and corroborative testimony, proving not only that Fitch did give the pistols that night, but that shooting at engineers was an old, long pursued, and favorite pastime to many of these defendants.

Caswell and Wells prove that Fitch gave them pistols to shoot at the engine house. D. J. Holden, p. 172, says:

"Heard the report that Fitch had hired some one to burn the depot in Detroit, and that he handed certain pistols out of the window to Wells or Laycock, to shoot the cars; asked him about it; he told me he did hand the pistols out of the window to them, mentioning either Wells or Laycock, or both, but either said they were not loaded or that they were only loaded with powder, and that he handed them out for them to fire at the cars merely, to frighten the engineer and alarm the road."

Can anything be more direct and positive than this? A plain, positive admission of all that is material in this cause for the point is not now to prove intent to murder, but to show that shots were fired with intent to so alarm engineers and frighten passengers, that this company, would be compelled to abandon its business. Again, B. Culver and Mrs. Hargrave prove that Laycock admitted to the same effect. Mr. Huntington, a witness omitted by the counsel, p. 78, says:

"I know Minor Laycock; heard him say he went to Fitch and asked for guns, and Fitch asked him what he wanted of them; he told him he wanted to shoot the cars. I told him I thought he would get into trouble, and he said there was no danger as there was no shooting that time, but said there was afterwards."

Does the testimony of Wells or Caswell go farther than this? Not so far, for here we have it by a witness of high character, that, although, the design of shooting at the cars was not carried out that night, *it was* subsequently. Again, Mr. English, another witness overlooked by the counsel, says, at p. 121:

"I know Fitch; worked for him in 1849; one day, at his house, he said he had laid a plan to fix the road, so that the company would not be able to hire an engineer within one year from that time to run the road; asked him why; he said because they would be afraid of their lives; he also said, "If they knew when Brooks was coming over the road, he never would be able to get through to the end of the rout."

You perceive, gentlemen, this shooting at engineers was not the impulse of a moment in 1850; it was an old and well matured plan. Again, Mr. Henry, another witness overlooked by the counsel, at p. 98, says:

"I remember whenguns were fired at the cars in 1849; I heard the cars pass, and heard the guns in the direction of the cars; there were four or six reports; think it was in the last of May or first of June 1849, 9 or 10 P. M.; I saw Corwin next morning and talked about the firing of the guns; asked him if they were firing at the train last night, and he said, "yes, I suppose so;" I asked him if anybody was killed, and he answered "no;" I said bye and bye they will kill somebody; he replied, d—n 'em if they don't want to be shot let 'em pay for the cattle they have killed; I told him that was a bad idea, and they would kill innocent people who paid their money for riding over the road; he said 'd—n 'em they need not ride over the road if they don't want to be killed.'"

Thus you see, that even in '49, Fitch was not the only one who was identified with this practice of shooting at Engineers. How readily Corwin knew that the shots were fired at the cars, and how freely the threat of killing and shooting flowed from his lips! What difference does it make then, whether Wells is true or false? He is true in this at least, for all he proves, and more too, is proven by witnesses against whom counsel dare not hazard a breath of suspicion.

Counsel has dwelt much upon the testimony of *Amanda Fitch.* The counsel feels no more kindly to her than I do. I would not hurt that child for a thousand worlds. I sincerely wish she may never have to fill a witness' box again; and hope, the present cloud passsing from her young brow, her future may be one of cloudless brightness. But what is her testimony, gentlemen? It is the strongest corroboration of the evidencc adduced by the prosecution. She says that Wells and Lacock came to the window; asked Fitch for his pistols, and also for some paper; that Fitch gave them, without asking what they were for, or uttering a single word. A tale, gentlemen, the truth, of which I need not question; as it is utterly inconsistent with any other hypothesis, than that there was pre-arrangement between the parties to come there for the pistols. If the prosecution had known that she would give such testimony, the unpleasantness of obliging her to testify against her friends, could scarce have excused them from placing her on the stand. I do not now stop to answer the charges of perjury, made against Wells: they are easily answered; but why do it, when he is only one among the many who prove this fatal point? You will remember these pistols were favorite dragoon pistols of Fitch; that Amanda says he never loaned them before; and yet, that he loaned them to a rude boy, in the dark of the evening, without a single word of enquiry!

I have now, gentlemen, gone through with each act mentioned in the list which purported to give all that were in proof; and you cannot fail to perceive what an entirely different character they assume, and how many more are identified with them, when the entire testimony is read, and read from the full report, instead of carefully prepared abstracts. I will now proceed to add to the list some *ten* others, important ones, too, which have escaped the attention of counsel, or at least have not been placed in this connection, where alone they can have their just force and strength.

28.—Mr. Spaulding, p. 67, says: "I remember the time when the locomotive "Dexter" was run off east of Mich. Centre, on the dry marsh, some eighty rods east of the Centre; it was in June, 1849; myself, Otis Kingsbury, and J. M. Hewitt were on the locomotive; it was drawing a train of racks, loaded with R. R. timber, going west, in the P. M.; we were running on the passenger trains time. After we got to Leoni, we run very slow for a while, and then increased the speed to get out of the way of the passenger train which was expected; I discovered a stick of timber ahead, but could not stop the train; we struck the obstruction, and it was cut in two, and did not throw off the train; I stopped the train after running some forty rods, the other two men jumped off before we struck the timber."

The witness goes on to state, that when the engine was stopped, Fitch, Filley, and some others came up. I will not detain you by reading the entire of this evidence, as it is lengthy, but ask your attention to the following portions: "Fitch said, "Spaulding, what's the trouble?" I think I told him some d——d hyena had put a timber on the track, but we had not run over it. Fitch said "Spaulding, by God, the Company never can run this road in safety, until they come out and pay us our price for killing cattle and damages done to other property." I said I could not see why the obstruction was placed, at that time, unless it was intended to catch a passenger train, as they did not know this train was coming; there were some remarks made like this—"probably the men who put it there, knew their business." I said if it had got to that pass, that we could not do our business on the road, I, for one, was ready to come out and defend the road with arms, if necessary. Fitch said if that was it, they might come on; he had at his house two double barreled guns and some pistols loaded, ready for business, and they had men enough to use them."

I will not detain you longer, by reading the description given of the dry marsh. You cannot have forgotten it—your blood like mine must have chilled, as you heard that witness detail that it was thro' God's Providence alone that the engine was not flung into the terrible abyss; that if the passenger train had come along first, its more rapid speed would infallibly have turned it from its course, and dashed it down deep into that slime, through which shafts have been sunk with ease over fifty feet without finding its bottom.

But the counsel will ask, where is the evidence to convict Fitch and Filley with this offense? I answer, you find it in their expressions to that gray haired man, as he stood on the occasion trembling and breathless—"Spaulding, by God, the Company can never run this road in safety, till they pay *us*."—"Probably those who put it (the obstruction) there knew their business." Is this, gentlemen, the language that would at such a time flow from hearts of men "who had never violated any law of their country?" The picture presented, was terrible, and needs no gloomy coloring. The catastrophy which a kind Providence had averted, was fearful, even to contemplate. Fancy that doomed train approaching, with its precious freight—families returning from long and painful absence—visions of home and happiness flashing before them; on they rush, unconscious of the fate prepared for them; there is a sudden stop—one mighty bound of the engine—one shrill whistle—one wild scream, and all is over. They are sunk, entombed—not in the beautiful cemeteries where mourning friends may weep over their ashes—not even in the bright, clear waters of our lake; but amid the slime and mud that ages have accumulated in that dismal spot. Of a truth, gentlemen, these men might say, they "knew their business," for they had learned it fearfully and well. Such was the fearful picture presented to their minds. It was one calculated to shake the firmest nerve—to appal the stoutest heart; but it shook, it appalled not them; their minds had brooded over it; familiarity had robbed it of its terrors, and it only called up the old motto of their hearts and mouths—"by God, the Company can never run their road, till they pay for our cattle." Their actions, their language, their demeanor, were all those of guilt. I confess, gentlemen, that if this fearful deed was shown by any ordinary evidence, my mind would be loth to receive it. It would seem too fearful, too improbable; but it *was* done—some one did it—the only question is, who? And who so likely as those who often threatened to do it?—who, in that fearful hour gloated over it?—and even amidst the kind manifestations of Providence, yelled forth their demon threats? But this is not all.

Spaulding further says: "The same time I found other obstructions on the track near Filley's house; they were old strap rails driven into the joints of the rails. They were placed in along for 60 rods, some right opposite Filley's house and Fitch's garden. There was generally a bush thrown before the obstruction to cover or hide it from us; once found a dead calf drawn on the track—the obstructions were well calculated to throw a train off—some of them were within 30 feet of Fitch's house—the track within 20 or 30 feet of Fitch and Filley's houses, any one coming out from Fitch's, towards where the men were when they came to the engine, must have passed right over and among these obstructions on the track."

29.—Sherman, at p. 55, narrating a conversation between himself, the two Prices and E. Champlin, says: "Price told of a plan laid for Wescott; said Wescott had been in the habit of coming to the Centre and playing cards; the plan was to place a seat so that Wescott would sit at the window, and they would stone him through the window from the outside; those inside, at a signal, were to blow out the lights and jump away, when they were to smash Wescott's head with stones from the outside; this was told in presence of Champlin and the other Price; said they knew he was a spy, and he ought to be killed; this was the plan they had laid, and said if he had come again, they would have killed him. I spoke to Wescott, and warned him. Had also heard Corwin threaten to shoot Wescott, if he had come down at night."

Wells also proves that he heard of the same plan.

Wescott, at p. 88, says: "I heard of a plot to assassinate me at the Centre; I went to the Centre to find out what was going on; I crawled through a hole under the bar-room floor; it was in the evening, in Nov., and the Price boys, Wm Corwin and Credit, were in the room. I remained under the floor a short time, and Fitch came in; I heard the Price boys say they were d——d fools for letting me slip through their fingers; that I was the only man that could injure them, and that they had made d——d fools of themselves in confiding so much to me, and I must be laid out. They spoke of a former plan which failed; and said among themselves there must have been a traitor in the camp, or I would have taken the seat they designed for me.

"I had on a certain occasion been invited in the morning to come down in the evening and play a game of eucher; I went down and found Jack Freeland, Corwin, Prices, two Champlins, Barrett and N. Credit—Filley came in, and said every thing was ready to play eucher in the other room, and invited me to go in; and wanted me to take the seat next the window, looking out on the stoop. I did not do so, as I had been apprised that if I did, my life would be in danger."

And in the face of such testimony as this, we are asked where is the proof of combination among these defendants?

30.—Wescott proves that one night he was chased through a creek. Wells proves that he heard Filley tell Fitch he chased a spy through the creek, the same night. And Sherman, p. 54, says E. Champlin told him of it.

31. In May, 1850, a stick was placed in a culvert so as to strike the cars: this was in the evening and a different occasion from that already refered to. Freeland admitted that he saw it but passed on lest should be laid to him—proved by Spaulding.

32, At page 88, Wescott says:

"I remember once when Fitch predicted the cars would be detained; I came down in the morning to take the cars for Detroit, and Fitch said I need not look for the cars until the sun got over past the meridian; they were then due from the west; it was soon after sunrise in the morning. He said it in reply to my remark that the cars were rather behind their time, the cars did not come along that day until near 6 o'clock P. M.; it was the day the cars were run off at Galesburg, and that caused the delay."

The counsel was wise not to present this testimony in any appropriate connection, for even his sophistry could scarcely explain away the miraculous manner in which Fitch could foretell so improbable a thing, as that the cars due at sun rise, should not come till evening. Clearer proof of a guilty foreknowledge of that outrage could not be adduced.

33. Lake proves that in March Doct. Farnham told him Fitch had hired Mount and Ackerson to burn the depot at Jackson, and that Williams told him the same, and that Mount and Ackerson also told him they were to do so. Caleb Loud at page 74, states he met Corwin in the same month, and says:

"We were riding round the sheds by the Depot at Jackson when I remarked that a fire there would sweep the whole lower town. He put his hand on my arm and said, "Just remember my word, there will be one here before long."

Is there no evidence of concert here? Mount and Ackerson are employed to burn: how does Corwin know there will be a fire there soon? Is it not here and in every instance, manifest that whoever might do the deeds, all were privy to it, aiding and encouraging?

Wescott at page 86 says: Fitch spoke of the burning of Depots as part of their plans, and that Filley once "spoke of burning the depot at Jackson; proposed to Corwin to burn it; said he had been by it and saw a good many shavings there which would make the work easy." At page 35 McMichael speaking of his interview with Corwin in Sept 1850, says:

"He wanted I should go in with him and help to tear up the railroad track; he also wanted I should help him to set fire to the depot of the railroad at Jackson; he said we should be well paid for doing it; he said Fitch would pay us; he said he wanted to injure the Co. all he could, that they run over cattle and would not pay for them;"

The enrire truth of this witness is established by Morgan Wescott page 118, who overheard the conversation by chance, and corroborates every particle of the testimony. Entirely unimpeached witnerses, men against whom not a word had been said even by counsel, proved every material point. We have the burning of depots fully established as one of the many designs of the defendants both before and after the fire in Detroit.

34. This is oné of the most remarkable of all the designs of the defendants indicating as you will perceive, combination, perseverance and scientific skill. Brown, at page 39, says:

"Heard Jack Freeland once say there could be a plan fixed to blow the cars up; this was when he was dropping in clover seed on Filley's hill. Joseph Wells and I were together when he said so. It was thus: To conceal powder so fixed that it would explode when the cars run over it; he said this was a plan talked of, and that it could be done at the dry marsh; he said he knew it would work, and when they passed there tt would blow them off the track."

and Charles Rogers page 117, says:

"Heard Fitch talking of the cars; he said by placing a keg of powder under the track, and having a trail of powder to the track, it could be fired by means of percussion matches under the rail; said he would like to see it done; have heard him speak of damages by the road in killing cattle, in justification for the depredations."

Wells testifies to the same conversation as Brown, and Caswell says he heard Fitch speak of it. You will bear in mind that this testimony, refered to early in 1850, Freeland had but a crude idea of it; he contemplated the effect, but had little notion of the means. Fitch, more intelligent, improved somewhat on the idea, he thought of percussion caps, but still, that was far from the best and most certain means of causing the explosion. We next hear of this scheme by Phelps and Lake, who say Doctor Farnham showed them a machine for blowing up the cars; that Fitch spoke of it to them; they described the construction with three tin tubes, and state that the Doctor told them he had some trouble before he could make an explosive composition to suit him for it, but had at length succeeded. Now, then, we have Freeland's crude idea, at length brought to perfection. It has received the finishing touch and is now prepared to murder on scientific principles. But the counsel will say, *that* is the testimony of Phelps and Lake. I promise that at the proper time I will show you conclusively that Phelps and Lake are entitled to full credence, but for the present I can dispense with their tesiimony. All they prove is proven by others. Asa Wyman whom you will remember as a very unwilling witness for the prosecution at page 58 says;

"I know Doctor Moulton, on trial; had a talk with him about railroads; he said he had heard they were going to blow up, either "a road" or "the road;" don't know what road he refered to."

Now although this testimony at the time it was given occasioned much laughter, does it not show in connection with the other evidence, that Moulton was cognizant of this Freeland plan? They would have no secrets from one who was to burn a depot for them; and can you doubt what road was meant, or that he referred to the very machine mentioned by Phelps. Asa Burdick on page 109 and 110, says: "I know Dr. Farnham; I was in Jackson last spring; in March or April saw the Dr. going into a grocery formerly kept by Showers, a country gent.; Corwin called the Dr. up and treated him, and then whispered and talked privately together; we went out together towards Bascom's Hotel;—took me one side to an alley, and said, I want to tell you something, for I believe you to be a pretty d—d good fellow. Think he was pretty well corned; he then said—the railroad—and here halted a moment, and then continued—hell and damnation! the roailroad will all be blown up in less than a month."

"The Dr. said $10,000 all gone to hell in one minute: said also, he had the tools to do it." The old fellow was pretty well corned when he said it.

Even in their drunken ebulletions, the fullness of their hearts came forth.

Nether Phelps nor Lake prove more than this. The testimony is natural, and apart from the fact that it is given by men of high unblemished character, has truth stamped upon it, and shows a deadly settled enduring combination between Fitch, Freeland Moulton and Farnham. Dobbs on page 119, says: "In a conversation he had with Williams, Myers, and Corwin, "they said they wanted another hoist, and spoke of powder; said if that wouldn't do they would try semething else."

35. Taylor proves that in July '50, the cars were stoned,—he went to the door—Williams and Woliver passed him towards Filleys and he heard one of them say he had stoned them, and would do so while he remained at the Centre.

36. Two wood piles were burned at the Centre. Huntington, who with Stone, put the fire out, says at page 79: "Fitch, Filley, E. Champlin and Mr. Broniger, came up to us. Mr. Stone told those who come up we had a hard night's work, and called on the cars for help, and they only stopped and gave them a damning and went on. Champlin said that was right, we ought to be d——d, and d——m those who would'nt d——m us. Filley said we ought to be burnt up with the wood, then the company would pay our wives half price for us. They blackguarded us for putting out the fire and watching the road. I told them I thought it was my duty to save property when it was being destroyed." "While we were putting the fire out we heard walking and whispering in the bushes near us but could see no one."

Mr. Stone says: "Fitch, Filley and Champlin came there about daylight when we were putting the fire out. I told them I had been to Jackson for help, and also stopped the cars to get help. Fitch replied I ought to be burned up with it and the road would pay my wife half-price for my ashes."

It may be doubted if this is proof that Fitch, Filley and Champlin fired the wood, but their expressions would lead to that conclusion. Why were they there before day-light? Not to render assistance. Their expressions show them capable of the act; and their presence, their means of doing it. Who were the persons heard in the bushes? None but these were seen at any time.

37. Mr. Dobbs, a witness who stands entirely unimpeached before you, says page 119 and 20: "At Hadden's grocery, Williams, Corwin and Myers were present, Williams asked me if I wished to

go into a speculation to make some money: told him I did; he asked me if I knew where the steamers Mayflower and Atlantic laid up; I told him I did not; that Ward's boats, I believed, generally laid up at Newport.

He said there was a speculation to be made, that they wanted those boats to be brought to the water's edge; said to me, you know al about the arrangements about the boats, and there is $500 ready for you if they can be burnt. I told him I thought it would be a bad speculation; he said my expenses would all be borne, if I had to go to Buffalo, I could live like a gentlemen; said if I succeeded, I could have $500, and he would refer me to the best backers in the county for the $500; spoke of Fitch, Filley and E. Champlin."

Here are three of the defendants, contemplating burning as a means of bringing the company to terms, and referring to three others as willing to aid them.

38 Holmes, page 97, testifies that Williams for no other reason than that he was suspected of being a spy, assaulted and beat him in the most brutal manner. He thus describes the injuries he received: "And I instantly received a blow on my head which knocked me senseless for some time, and paralyzed one side of my head so that I have lost the use of one side of my tongue—it broke my jaw, and I was disabled for some time from the blow. I think Filly, E. and L. Champlin, and Kirkendall were present."

At page 101, John H. Dexter says: "A short time before, I heard Fitch, Filley, Corwin, Prices and others speak of Holmes being a spy; heard Corwin tell the way H. was struck with the bottle; said Williams held up the bottle, and he struck it out of his hand, and it struck Holmes. I heard W. call H. a spy just before the blow; I was present when H. was struck, but did not see the blow; the bottle passed clear by my head, and went very swift; it could not well have been thrown swifter."

I ask you gentlemen, to give this occurrence its full weight. Can the mind fancy a more brutal deed, than this cowardly attack by a young and powerful man, upon an old and feeble one—whose only offence was being suspected as a spy. If there was no combination why this restless dread, this bitter hatred of spies, that breaks forth on every occasion from the lips of these defendants? Every man who did not belong to the combination was suspected and treated accordingly—even Holmes, weak, poor, feeble, tottering on the verge of the grave, could not escape their suspicions and their fury. When we find an old man thus stricken down and almost murdered by brute force, upon suspicion alone, it is fearful evidence that the menace against spies "to kill and shoot them," were not idle words but settled purposes.

I have now gentlemen, gone thro' a fair and candid list of aggressions, comprizing most, but not all of those committed. Altho' I felt as I proceeded that I must have been dull and tedious, you will admit that I could not otherwise have removed the impression that must have been made on you by an able and ingenious argument. A fair and full reading of the testimony was the most direct and convincing answer to that argument, and casting aside every attempt at sophistry and eloquence, such is the answer I have given.

You will remember that when the eloquent counsel concluded his list of menances overt acts, he gave this as the result: they numbered twenty-seven in all. Filley was compromised in four of them; Corwin in six; and the Prices in three; and no other defendant was identified with any of them. I need scarce claim that the list I have presented is fuller and more accurate; you see that it is. It is more candid for I have not read the evidence from prepared extracts, but from the full report with by means afforded you to judge if I erred; and mark how widly its result differs from his. Instead of 27, I have 38 menaces, or overt acts; and the following defendants are clearly compromised in the following number of the 38.

Fitch in 19; Filley in 17; one or other of the Prices in 11; Corwin in 15; one or other of the Champlins in 7; Williams in 7; Tyrrell in 1; Farnham in 2; Lemn in 1; Barrett in 1; Freeland in 3; Laycock in 1; Credit in 1; Mount in 2; Ackerson in 1; and Myres in 1. And had time parmitted I might add still further to the list.

When the learned counsel from his long research could only find implication of three defendants, each in only a few instances, we cease to wonder at the fact that he has also been unable to perceive how these repeated acts of aggression, in their number and manner of performance, indicate concert and combination. I will not say "none are so blind as those who will *not* see," but I do think, your views will be very different from his.

And now gentlemen, permit me to ask in all reason, do we not find the evidence of full concert and combination in these acts and the declarations that accompanied them? I do not ask you to look at *any sidgle one of them* only, but look at them *all*, and answer upon your solemn oaths do you believe there was combination? You will remember that concert need not be proved by written papers nor by even parol agreement—nor by any single transaction. The authorities I have read show, and the court will I hope, charge you that combination can be proven, by different acts, done by different persons, if there is concurrence in time, in motive, kind and object. In these acts we have all these concurrences, the uniform threats of those committing them is to injure the road; the uniform object to be effected is the same; and almost every single act is accompanied by a declaration of the same motive, which has been so often rung in our ears; "the road must be compelled for cattle killed."

What is the nature, scope and object of the combination charged against these defendants? simply this, that there was an understanding between them that for the purpose of forcing the road to pay for cattle, they would at all times and on all occasions do what injury they could to the road; and that in the perpetration of these injuries, and, in the event of arrest or trial, they would aid and encourage each other; we do not claim that there was ever a positive distinct meeting of all the defendants where it was agreed to do any one particular act; such pretence or proof is not necessary. The combination we charge is clearly proven, when we find sixteen of the defendants, for a space extending over two years, constantly engaged in acts of aggression springing from the same motive and aiming at the same end; when we find the perpetrators of these aggressions freely communicating their crimes to the others, and receiving praise and encouragement; the freest confidence prevailing among them upon these subjects; when we find each one, at all times, ready upon the slightest intimation that opportunity offers; to engage in any, even the most fearful and appalling aggressions, these things are clearly proven, and they exclude every other hypothesis save this—that these men acted in concert; that there existed between them a firmly knit and fearful union; that they were actuated by the same motive and aimed at the same end.

The extent and scope of that combination is also shadowed forth in these acts and menances, within them are comprized obstructions of the trains, shooting at engineers, stoning the cars, burning culverts, burning depots and burning boats. One other observation gentlemen, and I pass from this branch of the case. The only witnesses for the prosecution the counsel for prisoners pretended to assail or discredit, are Lake, Phelps, Wescott, Woliver and Wells: now, you may *strike* out all the testimony of these witnesses, and with the exception of a few of the most venial acts, the proof in relation to the acts I have read continues just as conclusive and implicates just as many of the defendants.

But if further evidence were needed that a combination existed among these men, of the character I have described, we find it in the meetings at Filley's. I will not weary you, by reading the mass of testimony, in which the character of these meetings is described. I will only read to you the testimony of Brown, who you will remember stands entirely unimpeached, and whose integrity is expressly conceded. Brown, page 38 and 39, says:

In April, 1850, became acquainted with the most of them; was then living with Ami Filley, at Michigan Centre; now reside in Jackson village; went to live with Ami Filley in April, 1850; I lived with him about two months; was employed to work generally for him; he then kept public house; frequently saw those persons meet at Filley's: could not identify the times, but they met often; sometimes in the day time and sometimes at nights; at nights they would generally stay till 10, 11 or 12 o'clock, and some would stay all night at times; Fitch never stayed all night; Welsh I have seldom seen at Filley's; Moulton and Penfield were not so often there as the others; Ackerson was not there generally at the time of meetings; came as any other person; the others met there habitually and often.

Have heard Filley speak of R. R. Co. at these meetings; have heard Filley say that he could have no feelings or sympathy for this Company; heard him say that people who traveled on it had better be cautious, they had been warned not to travel on it; have heard threats that they would let them (the Company) know there was a God in Isræl; they did not say particularly how they would let them know it; have heard Jack Freeland, Mr. Fitch, and Mr. Filley say something about God in Israel; have also heard them speak of the dry marsh; have heard them say, Mr. Filley in particular, that the dry marsh would be a good place to let them off the cars; they allowed it would be a good place to let the cars run off.

Freeland, Fitch and Filley, said they had warned persons not to travel on the road; don;t recollect they said anything in particular of hand bills, but said they had warned them; they said they wanted the road to pay up for cattle killed, &c. The persons I have named, talked the above matters freely among themselves, but shut up before strangers; when they have been talking so and have seen others coming, they would not continue the conversation if the new comers were not connected with them.

At page 100, Dexter, whom you will remember was a stranger, no way associated with the defendants, but who worked for Filley, says:

" At their meeting, when I came in, they appeared to change their topic of conversation." You will remember that Wells, Woliver, Dixon and other witnesses, describe these meetings more fully, and testify that the sole topic of conversation was the railroad. What are the elements of combination? Unity of motive, purpose and design, make the fullest combination. Are not all these evidenced by the habitual meetings and the constant discussion of one unvarying subject. How can you judge the intent of men if not by their language, and if words mean any thing, those used at these meetings evince unity of motive to extort payment for cattle, and unity of object to injure this company in every possible way; this is combination and for an unlawful purpose. But we are told there was never an appointed meeting. It is perfectly immaterial how they came together. When together,their language shows that the same hatred of this road burned in every breast; that the same felonious designs were brooding in every heart. We are told there never was an unlawful meeting. Gentlemen, modern days have given birth to many strangeg ideas, but it is among the strangest and most fearful when a distinguished lawyer before a high tribunal, and to an empannelled jury, says in the face of testimony like Brown's (and he is conceded to be a truthful witness) these meetings were not unlawful—what, gentlemen, not unlawful to warn travel off this road—not unlawful to plan and suggest the precipitation of whole trains into the dry marsh (a thing afterwards attempted)—not unlawful to threaten and agree to let this company know there was a God in Israel. For the last three months we have been learning the Leoni vocabulary and know what that expression means. It calls up terrible pictures of property destroyed, lives endangered, and snares for the coming engine. But men may do these things,provided they do not issue public calls, appoint a chairman and secretary, they may come together concoct plans, agree upon arsons, and have at least, one authority upon which to tell courts and juries it is right and not unlawful.—Gentlemen, there is no need of a chairman and secretary to make an unlawful meeting, there is no need to show *all* the defendants at one meeting to prove combination, and though counsel tells us they had no tyler at the door, the evidence tells us they had one in every heart. "They talked freely among themselves but shut up before strangers," "when I came in they appeared to change the topic of conversation." Yet you are told the meetings were public, there was no tyler at the door. But says counsel they met casually and at different places. Yes gentlemen, but whenever and wherever they met, the railroad, and plans to injure it was the burthen of their speech, they did not want notice to come prepared to speak of that, it was ever present, they were ever ready; they did not need a chairman to announce the object of the assemblage: the purpose of the combination was single, well defined and fully understood; its members were well known to each other, and whenever or wherever they met, each knew that this would be the most acceptable and interesting subject to the other.

Bnt, geutleman, if acts and meetings do not show combination, take a few individual expressions, proved by witnesses not sought to be impeached in any way. Holden and Galespie, page 73 and 74 prove:

"Gardner spoke of the cars being stoned the night before; Fitch replied that it was very mild means they were now using; if they did not pay for cattle killed they would get something worse than stones; said it would cost the road $100 for every animal killed."

This, of course, contains no allusion to others.

Monroe, page 78. "Freeland said, they had better pay for the cattle; they were all opposed to the road for ten milles back; if spies had been along the night before, they would have got blown over; he would shoot one quick as a squirrel; had a gun and kept it loaded for that purpose." Knickerbocker, p. 96, says: "Fitch said he considered the course, the people were taking, justifiable; they had their cattle killed and could obtain redress in no other way. Judges could be bought, &c." There was no combination, there was no identity of object. Yet *the people* were laying obstructions to obtain redress—community of motive, act and object, but no concert. Welling, p. 110, says:

"Fitch made an estimate of the cattle killed, by the road, near Leoni, and said there had been forty head killed, and that they had already cost the company over $400 apiece. Burnet told him he had better tell the boys they had gone far enough, and that a little labor or a few words from him (Fitch) would stop the depredations. Fitch replied that he told the boys to get pay for their cattle if they could, if they could not they must lay their plans so as not to get caught at it."

Of course "the boys" were imagined persons. It was mere fancy in Burnett to suppose Fitcu was the controlling leader, and a mere idle jest in Fitch to say he had given such advice to imaginary persons. Yet there may be some truth in this. These two defendants, you will remember, were on the committee appointed to confer with the Attorney General, and leaders are generally appointed on important committees. I refer you to the letter of Fitch to Mr. Brooks.

"Michigan Centre, Oct. 29, 1849.

"Mr. J. W. Brooks—Dear Sir:—Almost every day some persons wish to take passage on the cars at this place, but the trains refuse to stop for them. Yesterday Mr. G. C. Chatfield, mother and sister wished to take the cars for Detroit and gave the usual signal, but no notice was taken of them. Now, if this policp coms from you or your legal advisers, as did the insulting half-pay proposition for killing cattle, if serious accidents do occur on the road, on your head, and yours alone, must rest the responsibility.

Yours, &c., Abel F. Fitch."

And ask you to apply to it the following languege taken from the charge of an eminent judge: "It frequently happens that unnecessary, strange and contradictory declaratious cannot be accounted for otherwise than by the fatality which attend guilt, Apply the same rule to Fitch's prophesy that the cars would be late the day they were run off at Galesburg. I refer you to the "Price Boys Warning" so often alluded to, signed "By order of the Committee." Dowdle, p. 110, says he asked Penfield what the Leonians were threwing the cars off the track for; Penfield replied, "we are contending for our rights." But the counsel will tell you "we" is indefinite, it means anybody and therefore points to nobody. Nichols, p. 120,—Fitch, speaking of thase instructions, said: "They were the only means for bringing the company to tersm." *(Here Mr. Van Dyke read from the testimony of several other witnesses and continued.)* And so on gentlemen to the end of the chapter, I might detain you for hours reading similar expressions from almost every one of the defendants; but why waste your time on a part of the case so fully proved. I need not recall to your mind the constant expressions of all the defendants relative to spies—but I will ask you how came among these defendants this uniform hatred and fear of spies? How many of the defendants are proved to have constantly used threats against spies? Nearly every one. How many are uniformly found speaking of people being warned not to travel on the road? Nearly every one. How many are found speaking of the dry marsh? More than half of them. How many speak of the impossibility of conviction, and their readiness to swear for each other? Every principal one—Fitch, Filley, Williams, Prices, Champlin, Freeland, Corwin, who can prove that a "horse is a blacksmith shop, and every hair a candle!" and others whom I will not detain you by referring to.

I respctfully submit to you, gentlemen, that the proof of combination is perfect. We find it everywhere, It stands out on every page of the evidence. These defendants do not talk the language of men unconnected with others—on every occasion they speak the language of combination. Each one speaks in the plural, "we are contending for our rights." "I have advised the boys," &c. &c.—The same uniform ground of complaint is on the lips of each one—"they must pay for cattle." They meet habitually, discuss the same unchanging theme. At these meetings plans of outrage are suggested—they are afterwards carried into effect. We find most of defendants identified with these acts. We find others sustaining them, and if all this fails to prove combination, the entire law, relating to conspiracy, might as well be blotted from our books, for proof of it would be impossible. But combination is proved, and I feel satisfied there is no doubt remaining in your minds on that subject.

It is true, gentlemen, that Woliver, one of the witnesses who testified to the sayings and doings of these conspirators, has been assailed.—ed. The evidence of the acts and combination deducible from them is quite perfect without poor Woliver. But what is said against him? Why, that he is a poor worthless driviling sot. And who made him so? Who made him poor? Who robbed him of health and happiness? Who paid his year's labor by charging him for a barrel of whiskey? Who clothed him in rags, dashed every trace of God's image from his features, and filled his veins with fire, until every affection was scorched, every flower of youth blighted, every hope consumed, and until even his reason tottered on its throue? You have heard it all—and now this same Amrni Filley would tell you—"Don't believe this poor drunkard."

But, gentlemen, the guardian angel of Woliver had not quite left him. In a moment of bliss for him, he was led from the ruinous influences of Michigan Centre, made an effort to burst the toils that bound him! he has thus far redeemed his promises of reform; the blood is circulating once more in healthful current through his veins; life has once more smiled upon him, and the citizens of an interior village, who cheer him on in his new career, stand ready to vouch for his truth and good conduct.

WEDNESDAY MORMING.

The Court being in session, Mr. Van Dyke continued his argument as follows:

May it please your Honor and Gentlemen: I intend this morning, as briefly as the purposes of Justice will permit, to take up the alleged contradictions in the testimony of Wescott. I trust by a a candid and truthful review to show you that he is not impeached in a single material point—that his testimony is fully corroborated, and that he has sworn to nothing more startling or improbable than witnesses who stand before you unassailed. If I succeed in thic, you will be bound to give his evidence the weight and consideration which it merits.

I may not take up these alleged contradictions in the sama order in which they have been presented by the other side, but I will go thro' with them all.

1. It is claimed to have been shown that Wescott could not have got through the fence and heard the conversation to which he testified between Fitch and his wife. Whether he got *through* the fence, or passed over it, is perfectly immaterial. I will say but little on that point, for the material question is not *how* he got there, but *was* he thnre, and did he hear the conversation. You have seen the fence and can judge if he could not have passed inby the removal of one or more pickets. I think your recollection will tell you that at the very spot described by him there are several new pickets, and several old ones, the

nails of which appear to have been removed; but whether he got in thus or not is immaterial, and the witness may easily have been mistaken in his detail of a thing with which his mind was not impressed, or as to the spot where he entered on a dark night. The defence have sought to establish that at the time mentioned by Wescott, (the last of August) Fitch and his wife had their bed-chamber up stairs; this is material, ane if clearly established so far is an Impeachment. How is it established? Miss Fitch testified that at the time, and during all the warm weather, they slept up stairs; that it was their invariable habit to do so. Miss Beman says that she was at Fitch's on the 27th of August and a later period, and on both occasions they slept up stairs. Miss Clark also proved that up to September they roomed up stairs, but you will remember that on cross-examination she showed clearly that she was mistaken and had left Fitch's about the 22d or 23d of August. She says, "I still think it was about the middle of June, '50, I went there, and that I staid 9 weeks and returned to my father's." She in another place states that she went to Fitch's in the middle of June, and had $1 per week, and received either $8 or $9 at leaving. The best evidence of her intention to be truthful, is, that while she perceived her error she does not attempt to cover it up. At first she undodbtedly thought she was at Fitch's till September, probably that had been impressed upon her mind; but on the stand she fankly states other facts which she must remember better, and which show that she left there in August. I do not wish—it is not necessary that I should—attribute to the girl Amanda Fitch any intention to deceive. I can well imagine, without imputing to her anything that could soil the purity of her young soul, that while her child's warm emotions beat in sympathy with her father and stepfather, while her childish ear was keenly open to the sobs of her mother, it would be easy to bend her memory to her heart's wishes, and impress npon her willing mind the truth of any slight change of date or fact which might seem to tend to the relief of the peril and distress of her dearest and dearest friends. You are told she is young and candid. Concede it. She is not more so thon that other child Miss Clark; and if the latter was deceived and erred, how much more readily and naturally the former? Miss Beeman, the friend of Mrs. Fitch, the welcomed visitor at their house, is not infallible; and she, too, might err. Against this testimony, gentlemen, you have that of C. Burr, who proves that on the morning of the 29th of August, and on another morning a few days preceding it, he saw Fitch in bed in the *lower room*, and that on several occasions in August and September, when he called to see him, he came *partly dressed* out of that room. Also the testimony of Dr. Backus, the attendant physician of Mr. Fitch, that he most frequently visited him in the summer and fall, and his lodging room was always *below* stairs. But Mrs. Fitch was produced upon the stand though every lawyer must have known that her testimony on this point was incompetent. I will not say that she was brought here for effect or to move the sympathies of you or this crowded hall; but I will say she was *not cross-examined*. She passed in silence from the stand—she will pass in silence now. I would not to subserve any cause, indulge in reflections which might move her overtaxed sensibilities. May her sorrows soon pass, and happier and brighter days compensate her for the grief and gloom of the present. I will, however, say to the counsel that before he indulged in remarks upon this subject, and the exclusion of Mrs. Fitch's testimony, he should remember that he was the first to shut out the light by objecting to the proposal to prove by Dr. Backus, a gentleman of the very highest integrity, that Fitch admitted to him that he *had seen a spy under his bed-room window.* To contradict a witness,the proof must be as strong and clear as that which establshes an affirmative fact; but here, even if Wescott's testimony is disregarded, there is stronger, much stronger proof, that Fitch slept in the lower room, than that he did not at the time in question, and therefore the re is no impeachment.

2. The defence claim to have proved that Wescott could not have got through the hole under Filley's bar-room, and that hence his narration of the conversation there stated to be heard is false. I refer you to the testimony on this point. First there is the testimony of Hildreth. (Here counsel read Hildreth's testimony.) You perceive gentlemen, he only *thinks* he opened the hole 'tis true; but he did not measure it; but did not even notice it particularly, to ascertain its size; but *thinks* it was no larger in December than when he opened it.—Young Fitch proves that on Christmas day he tried to pass through the hole but could not. This might be; you were there and noticed that two large stones stand beside the hole; during the cold days of Christmas, it would be most natural that one or both of them should be placed in the opening, to exclude a portion of the air that would otherwise render the room over it unbearable. But in answer to all these doubts, we have the testimony of Mr. Clark, that in consequence of a communication from Wescott, he examined the hole and it was then as large as now. Knowing Mr. Clark's high reputation, knowing that you would believe every word that fell from his lips—counsel try to persuade you that he erred as to the date. There can be no error; he went examine in consequence of *Wescott's communication,* and from other testimony you can have no doubt as to what that communication was.

3. You are told that Wescott was indicted at Mackinac; to avoid the odium of it, he testified that Doctor Rankin, the prosecutor was himself indicted for perjury; fled and committed suicide to avoid conviction; but that the Company clerk of Mackinac, proved the Doctor never was indicted and died a natural death. Such is the statement made to you. (I refer you to Wescott's testimony, p. 95.)

"The indictment against me at Mackinac, was obtained on the affidavit of Jairus Rankin, before the grand jury. A *nolle prosequi* was entered, because Rankin was indicted by the same grand jury for perjury in making that affidavit. Wm. Gray was the prosecuting attorney. I went there for a trial three seasons, but he never appeared as a witness against me. I have been told that Rankin committed suicide."

You will perceive that Wescott does not say that Rankin committed suicide; he was only told so. You will also remember that it was stated by the prosecuting attorney, here in open court, that he had seen an account of the suicide of some Doctor Rankin, supposing he was the same Rankin, had mentioned it to the witness. By referring to the testimony of Mr. Kevan, the clerk of Mackinac, you will perceive that although there was no indictment found, a complaint was presented before the grand jury against Rankin, for perjury; a fact which might well lead the witness into the mistake. But this argument is needless gentlemen; the entire matter is immaterial in this case, and can only affect Wescott's testimony if he *meant* to deceive you. Did he mean to do so? If so, he certainly took a strange method, for unasked, he volunteers the statement that Mr. Gray was the prosecuting attorney; thus referring to my talented and cherished friend and colleague, a respectable member of this bar, *then in court*, and now at my side, and who from the official position he occupied, could give full and accurate information, thus furnishing a witness on the spot, to contradict him if he was false. As I review those alleged contradictions, they fade so rapidly under the application of the testimony, that I almost question if they were seriously urged.

4. It is stated to you that Wescott testified he saw Fitch and Dows *on Friday*, about 8 P. M.; go to the house of Gay, and it is claimed that this is contradicted by the testimony of Jones, Holden, Brown, and Sumner. You will remember that the Friday in question was February the 14th. On direct examination, at page 95, Wescott says: "I next saw them together, *about* the 12th of February, on Jefferson Avenue, on the corner of Woodward; I was dressed in disguise; they were conversing; they went from there to the house of Washington Gay, together." Although the report of the testimony does not contain any question and answer, you will remember that the defence, on cross-examination, tried to get him to fix the day as *Friday*, and, after some time, got him to say, at page 89—"When I followed Fitch and Dows to Gay's house, it was in the evening. I *think* this was on Friday. I was alone when I followed them." And this is all that is to be found on the subject. By referring to the testimony of Jones, you will perceive he does not pretend to account for Fitch on any evening. Holden saw Fitch on the 12th, soon after the cars got in. The witness then went, and got his tea; then went up town, was gone about *half* an hour and again saw Fitch on his return; thus leaving Fitch unaccounted for just at the hour mentioned by Wescott, (for you will remember the cars arrived about 8 P. M.) and for a sufficient time to go to Gay's.—Brown saw Fitch on the 13th, soon after the cars arrived; parted from him; got his tea; dressed for a cotillon party; and, about 9 P. M., again met Fitch, and attended the ball with him; leaving, on this night also, abundant space for the visit to Gay's. Mr. Sumner saw Mr. Fitch twice at a fair on Saturday night; but does not imply that he could not have gone to Gay's, as stated; for he does not name the hours when he met him; and, indeed, to even hint that he noticed the incomings and outgoings of any of the ruder sex, on an occasion when he was surrounded by the bright eyes of woman, would be an imputation which my very gallant friend, Mr. Sumner, would resent. We concede that the testimony of Brown excludes the idea that Fitch went to Gay's on Friday evening, the 14th, which probably accounts for the strong desire manifested to pin Wescott down to that day, on cross-examination. You perceive, then, gentlemen, that if Wescott had fixed the

date as either the 12th, 13th, or 15th, there would be no contradiction. Now, did he swear to the 14th? On his direct examination, when his mind was left free to its real impressions, he thought it was about the 12th, (Wednesday.) Goaded, on cross-examination, he said he thought it Friday. It is clear you cannot contradict a witness by dates or hours, when he only *thinks;* but it is clearer still, that, when he has two "thinks," you cannot select your choice one as his positive evidence, and contradict him on it. The presumption of law is the other way; it is in favor of a witness' truth. The whole of this matter, then, is, that the defence can say they came *very near* contradicting him. They were within a few days and a few "thinks" of it.

5. Wescott denied having used threats that he would yet see Fitch "peeping through the grates." Mr. and Mrs. Tull swears he did. We have to meet this as we best may; but I think there is little in it. Wescott may have used the threat, and forgotten it. You will remember that Tull fixes the time as the period when Wescott was accused of being a spy. It is very natural that, in the heat of the moment, smarting under the threats and abuse that were heaped upon him, he would return threat for threat; but what men say in hot, is often forgotten in cold blood. Again, gentlemen, if Wescott used those threats, and remembered them, why should he deny it? He was apprised that Tull and his wife were here to contradict him, and could easily have given some slight explanation, to break the force of their contradiction. If he never used the threats, or if he used them, and forgot exactly what he did say in the heat of passion, this does not impeach him. But the learned counsel tells you Wescott denied what Mr. Tyler proved, viz: that Wescott said—"A web was being woven round Fitch that would send him to State Prison." This, gentlemen, sounds serious. Ordinary threats, used in the heat of blood, amount to little; they are evanescent as the feeling that generates them. But here we have method—something that savors of the alleged counter-conspiracy; and how shall I answer it? Simply by telling you, gentlemen, that there is *no such evidence.* Neither Tyler, nor any other witness, swears to anything of the kind. Wescott was asked if he used these words to John Wells and Welch; he denied that he did; and there the matter rested. Neither Tyler, Wells, nor any other witness was called to contradict him. My answer is short, but it is complete—there is *no* such testimony. If there is, counsel are here; let them now point it out, or anything which looks like it.

6. You are told that while Wescott and Sherman testified that Fitch and Wescott were present at the fight in the ball alley, A. Cozier proves that neither Wescott or Fitch were at the alley till after the fight. By referring to the testimony of Cozier you will perceieve that he testifies to no such thing; on the contrary, he proves distinctly that Fitch and Wescott were about there at the time; if he did the oath of one witness could not impeach that of two—particularly when the defence, if they relied on this as a contradiction, could have fortified Cozier by J. B. Tull whom Cozier says was with Fitch, and who; altho' called to another point by the defence, was never questioned as to this. The failure to question Tull on this point is evidence that he would not say Fitch and Wescott were not at the fight, yet if

they were not, he should not have known it for he was with them.

7. You are told he is impeached as to the plan to kill him by stoning him through the window, because as counsel argues, the piazza from which the stones were to be cast is but three feet wide, and no arm in such a space could send a stone with sufficient force to do injury; and hence the whole story, yon are gravely told, is false. Gentlemen, you will remember this plot is not verified by Wescott alone. I yesterday read you Sherman's testimony, and you will remember that on this subject it is fuller and more minute than even Wescott's. You must believe him, for not a breath has been raised against his veracity, and while he and Wescott tell precisely the same tale, how are you to conclude that one tells the truth, the other speaks falsely? Again, if the argument of counsel was correct—if stones could not be thrown from the piazza, would it contradict Wescott? no, for he does not swear it could be done, he only tells such was the plan *of defendants*. But again gentlemen, tho' no athlete, I fancy that in three feet space (the piazza is four feet,) I could send a stone with sufficient force to do injury, aye, even to kill. But of this you can judge.

8. You are told, and told with all seeming seriousness, that he is impeached, because if the rules of evidence had permitted him to testify Mr. Harsha would have contradicted him '*by implication*,' so they came very near it again. I am glad that I am through with these alleged contradictions. As we have called them up for review divested of the imposing uniform and decoratiou in which the eloquence and imagery of couusel dressed them, they seem each one more ludicrous than its predecessor. A little more and thescene would better befit the after piece of the stage than a solemn trial for a high offence.

I have no doubts in assuming, gentlemen,that I have shown to your satisfaction that the alleged contradictions of Wescott are visionary; he is not contradicted in a single essential point. You remember his demeanor on the stand; it was frank. He gave his evidence clearly and without hesitation; he passed thro' a long and searching cross examination without the slightest material variance; altho' long a resident and well known in this community, no attempt was made at general impeachment. I might stop here, gentlemen, and require you to give credence to every word he uttered. Jurors are not at liberty to disregard testimony, when the witness stands fair before them without impeachmen, or contradiction. But I will go farther, gentlemen, I will take up a few of the most material points of this testimony and show you that in *them* he is fully corroborated by witnesses whom you dare not but believe.

He tells you the defendants were in the habit of meeting at Filley's discussing the sugject of the Railroad, and breathing threats against it. You have the same teslimony quite as strong as he gives it, from Brown, Dexter, Wells, and half a dozen others. He tells you that Fitch and other defendants said they had sent handbills, warning persons against traveling over the road. Attorney-General Lothrop, at page 158' and Chadwick, at page 107, testify to the same thing in equally strong terms, and so do other witnesses. He tells you that Fitch and others told him they were combined together to do all the injury they could to the road, that in effect, they had taken the law into their own hands,and were determined to bring the company to terms. Let your minds revert to the acts done, the conclusive evidence of combination which gathers round the proof of them, and you have from good and unquestioned witnesses, all and more than all that Wescott says. Look at the testimony of Attorney-General Lothrop on page 158, that Fitch and Burnett intimated there was no use in seeking redress at law, that obstructions were the only means left to bring the company to terms. Look at the testimony of Mr. Knickerbocker on page 96, where he tells you Fitch justified the obstructions, scouted the idea of having recourse to the established tribunals, and proclaimed that the money and influence of the company could corrupt alike the judges of the inferior and supreme courts. Again, Wescott tells you the scope and design of the combination at pages 85 and 86. He says that Fitch said, "if they could succeed in killing from 100 to 150 passengers during the Fair, it would bring the company to terms, if not, he wanted to know what in God's name would? If he failed in that, God damn them, we will burn them out. He also stated he would give me or any other person $1000 to burn four depots, viz: Detroit, Ann Arbor, Jackson and Niles, or that he would give $250 for burning either one of them. He said there were men among them who would do it, but thought it had better be done by some one not living at the Centre."

I confess, gentlemen, that here is something so fearful that the mind hesitates to yield it credence. But there is no accounting for the actions of men who begin by believing in the utter corruption of all who surround them, even of those whose virtue and wisdom have placed them to preside over the most sacred institutions; and who end by adopting vengeance as their guiding star, and hugging that hideous passion to their heart. They become blind to reason, justice and humanity. Every feeling turns to morbid hatred; every pulse throbs with bitter passion, and the innocent and guilty are alike sacrificed to minister to an insatiate appetite for revenge.

But we cannot refuse to believe merely because of the nature and horror of the crimes, Fearful and fiendish as this design is, it was attempted. You remember engine after engine was obstructed; you remember the testimony of Spaulding, that the obstruction at the dry marsh was intended for the passenger train, and that if it had come as expected, its hundreds of passengers would have sunk deep, deep into that hidden and hideous lake. You are asked is it possible that Fitch would design this deed, when he himself, and his family and his friends were passengers during the State Fair. 'Tis true they were at the Fair, but we find him and his family always on the day, never on the night train; and it was at night this fearful tragedy was to be enacted. But his friends. As to that portion of the argument I refer you to his own words to Chadwick, page 2f7, "my friends have been warned, and if they will ride over the road, *they must suffer the consequences.*" There is still the intention to burn depots. Is Wescott alone or uncorroborated in this? Is he the only witness who proves that the burning of depots was embraced in the designs of this combination? Not at all. Caleb Loud proves it. And is he a witness to be believed? Even counsel for defence do not question it. McMichael proves it, and his truth is undoubted. Morgan Wescott proves it, and his truth is unquestioned; and Dobbs proves that *burning boats* was also within the scope of their designs. These four witnesses stand fair before you, and you heard their testimony as I passed over the acts of aggression. They are not guilty of the crime of being employees of this Company; they are not polluted by any connection with "hated corporations." And it is not even claimed that grounds of disbelief have been presented against them. Yet they prove the very substance and essence of what Wescott proves; that fire, *fire*, was an instrument, the use of which was contemplated by these defendants. Wescott tells you again that it was part of the understanding of defendants, that they would, true or false, swear each other clear, and had friends of station and influence who would procure witnesses to swear to anything. Is Wescott alone in this? Have you not heard the same from other witnesses? Have you not seen it with your own eyes, heard it with your own ears? I will not imitate the distinguished counsel and tell you what Cooper would, but was not permitted to tell, but I will ask you, did not Hawley perjure himself? Was he not suborned to it, by a friend of these defendants? Was not that friend (the Rev. Mr. Billings) a man of influence? It is needless to weary you longer with this. I might go all through Wescott's testimony, and show that every line is corroborated; that he swears to nothing but what is corroborated by undoubted witnesses. I have referred to the most important portions of his testimony. I have shown you that he does not stand alone, but that corroboration comes in upon you from half a dozen other sources. I feel confident I have gone far enough to ensure credence for every word uttered by him.

Gentlemen, at this point I will ask you to pause for a moment and review the ground over which we have advanced. I have shown you by their acts, their assemblages; and repeated declarations, that these defendants had conspired to injure the Railroad Company, by breaking its cars—diverting travel from its line; stoning its trains, burning its culverts; shooting at its engineers; obstructing its engines; blowing up its track; and burning up its depots and other property, for the purpose, in their own language, of compelling the Company "to come to terms." I have shown you that these threats were not idle boasts or unmeaning outbreaks. What they *threatened* to do, invariably *they did.* I have shown you that every one of these defendants against whom a conviction is sought, was identified with the overt acts, many of which are of a character far more fiendish than the burning of a depot. All this has been established by witnesses, whose truthfulness is manifest and undenied. This is all proven, exclusive of the testimony of Wescott; his testimony (after the examination and analysis we have given) advances us one step farther; we find by him that it was contemplated to burn the Detroit depot; others prove it was contemplated to use fire—to burn boats and other depots; he advances the case to the mention of Detroit specially. This then is the position of our case.

The only thing yet remaining, is to identify these defendants with the fact. Gentleman, if an individual threatens to injure your business, assault your person, your property; and burn your house; if he is clearly identified carrying out the first three portions of his threats; and the house is burned by an incendiary, how much proof will you require to satisfy you that he is the man? Just so much proof do you want to be satisfied that these defendants are the persons who caused the depot in this city to be fired. So far we have advanced, and you will perceive that although these men are not now upon trial for expressions used and acts done in Jackson county; these expressions and acts, have, nevertheless, an important bearing upon the offence for which they are on trial.

Gentlemen, from time to time, as this trial progressed, much was said, and more felt, at the frequent and long delays which marked its history. The counsel for the prisoners, to escape from the responsibility which they cannot but feel must rest on them, for the unnecessary protraction of the proceedings, have, with well-feigned earnestness, turned round on the prosecution, and charged that we desired haste at at the sacrifice of their constitutional rights, and begged for stipulations to cover up the blunder of placing so many on trial at once.

Let this veil be removed, and let truth be apparent.

These defendants were placed on trial together, because it was evident that, if tried separately, and the mass of evidence adduced against each which would be competent from the nature of the case, no living man could foretell the end. And again, the defendants themselves *desired* a joint trial, to save longer durance in jail, and increased expense, as is evidenced by their *own consent and writing* on the files of the court. And yet counsel, in the very face of these facts, charge the joint trial as both an oppression and a blunder on the part of the prosecution.

If, indeed, defendants have ever been solicited to facilitate this trial at the sacrifice or risk of any legal or substantial benefit or advantage, then may they well throw back in our teeth our frequent censures of their long delays. But such is not the truth.

We respectfully submit that it is the duty of every one engaged in the administration of Justice, in whatever capacity, to avoid unnecessarily impeding its course; but, on the contrary, it *is* their duty to aid in rendering it as speedy as is consistent with the rights of parties litigant; that courts crowded with onerous duties should not be intentionally hindered; that jurors forced from their own business, interests, and homes, at severe sacrifices, and sometimes irreparable loss, should not be uselessly detained; and that expense, avoidable and unreasonable, should not be accumulated, to be wrung from the tax-payer; and that they who do these things have a fearful responsibility resting on their heads, especially if it be found that sickness and death ensue therefrom.

Gentlemen, I appeal to you for the truth of what I uow assert, for you were eye-witnesses. Every cause of delay which could subserve the purpose, has been seized upon with avidity by the defence. Was a prisoner temporarily sick, the defence would not stipulate to proceed, but doggedly stood still, and mockingly declared *their readiness* when the prosecution would produce the absent party. Was a juror unwell, and an offer tendered to have the testimony taken in his absence, and fully read on his return, it was rejected with contempt. And these scenes over and over again, when, too, the absent prisoner was one whose presence could afford neither information or aid to counsel; and when, too, the testimony proposed to be taken in a juror's absence, was of that character which would lose no force in being read to him from the minutes of the court.

Thus were we kept three long months; thus were you detained and annoyed a large portion of the time from Spring to Autumn; thus have expenses accumulated; the wheels of justice been clogged, and excitement kept up. So far as this defence had power or opportunity to effect it.

And to subserve what purpose? Was it to gather from the tamaracks of Indiana the Hawley's and Dyers of this defence? Was it that the Rev. Billings might cement the bond of friendship between Adams and his associates whose names stain or grace the annals of this defence? Was it that "cold inanimate nature" might be dragged forth from its *easily found* hiding place, to speak, not in the voice of *discovered* iniquity and confession, but on the originally hoped for "thunder tones?" Was it that tone might permit the preparation of elaborate tables, and ingenious theories of defence? or was it, worse, than an all, that death might in some chance blow end the deep and sure perils of this trial? Answer ye. And let counsel who have thus played this game with time, not now complain, if all has proved in vain; if *they* have had to drink the poisoned chalice to its dregs, and if they have again learned the severe truth that justice though slow is certain.

But for these most flagrant delays, consuming far beyond a full months time, this trial would have been ended long before serious disease or death overtook a single prisoner. Your verdict would have been rendered; these prisoners restored to liberty or confined to the penitentiary, where exercise, occupation, absence of uncertainty and excitement, and the fresher air would have preserved them in wonted health and vigor.

In view of these facts gentlemen, I ask you, how does it become the counsel for defence to speak of delays, or to wake up the dead, whose ghostly shadows should strike terror to their own souls.

And after all Gentlemen, perhaps, death although so feared and terrible, may even in its visitations in the course of this trial, have been kindness. Those whom it has touched with its fatal dart, are beyond the perils of this scene; beyond the dark shadows which seem to gather around its end; and if prepared, as counsel in time for the dread change "after lifes fitful fever they sleep well."

One can scarce look over this long list of defendants, and not sigh, that while yet in their childhood they had sank sweetly into their last repose, long before vice and crime had stained their youth, and subjected their manhood to this ordeal at the bar of their offended conntry. Then affection would have sung their last lullaby and kept their memories fresh in undying love. Now, God only knows their doom and their destiny. If that doom proves to be the Prison House, perchance the threats of vengeance, and the deeds of crime which have so long disturbed the nights, and desecrated the days of Leoni may cease. Punishment may effect its objects, security to mankind and reformation to the offender; and unadulterated good may ensue from this vindication of the laws.

But to return to the immediate matter upon which you are to decide. The Indictment charges that the depot was burned by Geo. W. Gay, wilfully and maliciously, the other defendants being accessories before the fact. Was the depot burned by an incendiary, and was Geo. W. Gay that incendiary? It is necessary that the prosecution should adduce evidence sufficient to satisfy you that the fire was not the result of accident, but the act of Gay. It is claimed that such evidence has not been adduced. Let us examine and see. I will not trespass upon your time by reading at length the testimony as to the position of the machinery, the condition of the depot, and the precautions taken to guard against fire. By reference to that testimony, you will find that all the machinery used was of the safest character; that no precaution against fire was omitted; that the building was so constructed, and the machinery so guarded that the superintendent, Mr. Brooks, a gentleman of vast experience and judgment in such matters, deemed insurance against fire unnecessary, and never did insure. You have the testimony of seven practical and experienced engineers and mechanics, experts, whose opinions are evidence, that in their judgment, the fire could not have been communicated by the machinery. Listen to a few of these opinions. Bear in mind that they come not only from experts but from men who were engaged about this identical machinery, and frequently examined it. Avery, page 21, tells you, "I do not think it possible for it, (the fire) to have taken from friction; that is now my opinion, and I thought so from the first." Frazier, page 20, says, "In my opinion there was no danger of fire from the friction of the machinery." Town, page 24, says, "In my opinion there was no possibility of its so taking fire." Ives, page 25, tells you that supposing the pulleys to revolve two hundreds and fifty times a minute, which is proven to be their greatest speed, he thinks there was no possibility of fire from them—they would not generate fire whether oiled or not, and he considered this machinery the safest he ever saw. Mr. Brooks and others testify to the same. Several of the same witnesses tell you that they repeatedly examined the journals, the only place where fire could generate, and never found them heated to any extent. Babbit's metal—constant examination—every precaution was taken against fire by the friction of the machinery, and it is really idle to dwell upon this branch of the proposition. The testimony is conclusive and utterly excludes the possibility of fire by friction. I will, however, call your attention to one other fact proven by Mr. Avery. There was but one pulley in the cupola, "and it ran the slowest of all." You will perceive then, that if we hereafter show that the fire originated in the cupola, it is idle to ascribe it to friction. But the counsel gravely tells you that Mr. Smith's mill was burned at Clinton. But turn to his testimony, and you find he says, "my experience is that elevators well constructed, and well cared for, cause no especial hazard, but not well attended to they do." It was scarce worth while to bring Mr. Smith sixty miles to tell us this. We were aware that elevators to be perfectly safe should be well constructed and properly attended to, and therefore gave you abundant evidence to satisfy you that this was so.

[Here Mr. Van Dyke read and commented upon the testimony of Mr. Brooks and others, and proceeded.]

But conceding that the machinery was all safe, we are told that there was the engine, and the fire might have been communicated by that. As matter of history the counsel told you there was a fire lately in Chicago supposed to have taken from an engine room, and read you a letter from the owner of the property, showing that his engine was placed and guarded in the same manner as the one in the Depot. Not a day after I received from Henry R. Williams, a gentleman well known to you, the letter which I now hold in my hand, stating that the owner of the property informed him he was satisfied the fire did not take from the engine, but was the work of an incendiary. Neither of the letters, gentlemen, is proper matter for your consideration, yet I am glad that the reading of the one called forth the other. It serves to warn us of the danger of going out of the case or paying the slightest attention to anything beyond the evidence. Now to return to this engine. What is it? Mr. Wood, page 26, says:

"I run a stationary engine; that is my occupation. I remember the fire at the depot. I run the engine at night. *That night it stopped a quarter before* 12. *The fire, before I left, was allowed to run down; he engine was pumped and everything secured.* To my knowledge it was not run again that night. Do not recollect that any *locomotive came into the building that night.*"

The only testimony upon this point, excludes the idea of the fire originating in the engine room. Here again, you will remember that if the fire first appeared in the cupola, it could not have proceeded from the engine, as the latter was on the first floor. But it is said it may have have taken from candles hanging on posts, or used in the bins on the second floor. Here is the testimony upon that point. Duncan Stewart who had the superintendence of that portion of the building, says:

"The workmen in the bins used candles in tin sconces. I was in the habit of going frequently about the bins at night to see that my orders respecting lights were obeyed. I believe they were delivering wheat on the night of the fire. I never but once saw a candle fastened by grease to the wood. I went up as the man was doing it. I never knew of its being done but once. I then stopped its being done. I had the nails placed for the sconces myself, so as to be out of the way of danger, and the men were not allowed to hang the sconces on any other nails."

And Daniel Stewart says:

"I was there when the work ceased the night before the fire; there was only one candle used there that night, *and I put that one out about a quarter before twelve.*"

There was no fire then from candles. Another chimera has fled before the evidence. But it is said that it may have taken from sparks issuing from the engine of a locomotive, passing through the depot below, or of some steamer passing in the river. The answer to this is easy. Every person who could be found who was near the building that night, has been on the stand, and all say that to their knowledge there was no locomotive in the depot, and no steamer fired up near the wharf that night. There is no evidence from the defence to raise such a presumption—the evidence of the prosecution negatives such an idea, and even if it did not, it is not for jurors to strain after imaginary and unlikely ones.

The Depot then *was* burned, and not through accident. It had long stood in its strength and usefulness. It was dedicated to a substantial and noble purpose; filled with the rich products of our soil, destined for the eastern market; and with the merchandize of our interior merchants. There it stood, a credit to our State; an ornament to our City. As we left for the East, it was the last sight our lingering eyes could *catch;* and as we returned, it was the first to greet our vision. On the evening of the 13th November, the autumn's sinking sun cast the shadow of this long and graceful building upon the rapid waters of our river; the midnight bell roused us from our slumbers, and hastened us toward the fated spot; but long before we could reach it, we could read its doom in the reddened sky, reflecting back the lurid flame. That costly structure, and all the accumulations of labor, enterprise and industry it contained, were enveloped in fire; the morning sun revealed to our sorrowing eyes, a vast heap of smouldering ruins; and this, gentlemen, was the work of an incendiary.

Who was that incendiary? Under the present Indictment, the prosecution was bound to prove to you that it was George W. Gay—and it has done so. But as all evidence on this point tends also to prove that he set the fire in the Cupola, it is necessary that I direct your attention to the proofs on that head. The prosecution does not wish, nor is it necessary to charge any want of truthfulnesss upon the witnesses produced by the defence to this point. The testimony of the witnesses on both sides, is quite consistent; there is neither necessity or propriety in imputing falsity to either. Some half dozen witnesses swear when they first saw the fire it came from the scuttle in the roof. Some eight others say when they first saw it, it was confined solely to the cupola—all agree that at some future period, the fire was in both scuttle and cupola. The only question then is, which saw it first; and where was it *then.* Each witness for the defence states he was aroused by the alarm of fire. Capt. Turner it was conceded, was the first who gave the alarm; he then was the first who saw it; and he tells you it was then a bright blaze in the cupola, not larger than a half bushel. Mr. Savinac, at whose door he first knocked, tells you he came to the door undressed; looked out; had a view of the scuttle; *there was no fire there, but there was in the cupola.* Mr. Rowland an Engineer in the fire department, tells you he got there before any Engine arrived; as a matter of duty ascertained where the fire was, to enable him to locate his engines when they arrived; the fire was *then* in the cupola, and *in no other place;* but some minutes *afterwards* he perceived it had extended to, and came out of the scuttle. Police Justice Higgins tells you, he commanded a view of the fire from his window; when he first saw it, it was confined to the cupola; he watched its progress, and saw it extended to the scuttle. Mr. McFarrand testifies with equal certainty and clearness to the same effect.—So do the other witnesses for the prosecution, all of them gentlemen of the highest character and respectability. And what other conclusion can you come to, than that the defendant's witness speak truly; they tell candidly what they saw; but they did not see the fire *until a later period* than the others, and after it had extended to the scuttle. As we review the evidence, we find that this point of the case looms up from it, clearly and firmly established.

Was Gay the incendiary who burned the Depot? It has been sworn by four witnesses that he said he was; and that he set the fire in the cupola. But first look at the probabilities. Gay lived in this City not a stone's throw from the Depot; he was where he might do it. We were told in the opening, that credible witnesses would establish the fact that for three weeks before, he was not able to move without crutches; but it was *not* proven; there was not a solitary witness—not even from Leoni, who could screw his courage to that sticking point; they did not even produce the crutches—though they were to be a part of the "mute inanimate nature." which was to overwhelm the prosecution. Gay then, could do it. He was familiar with the building, its construction, and its different parts; knew the hours and occasions when he could pass in, least noticed. He was just the man to be selected for such business. He was poor and needy. From early life, until he sank into the grave, he had revelled in scenes of licentiousness and crime. His name was a terror even among evil doers; he was shunned by the good—feared by the bad—an outcast with the mark of Cain upon his forehead. Did any desire to do a deed like this, Gay was a tool ready made and fitted to his hand. As somebody caused the depot to be burned, it is easy to believe that he was the tool used to do it. But there is still another item of evidence coming close upon direct and positive proof. A match similar to the instrument, (as I will hereafter show) by which this arson could have been, and in every probability was accomplished, was seen in his house, and in his possession. If murder is committed by means of a subtle and before unknown poison—if similar poison is found in the possession of a depraved person, capable of the crime, who had an opportunity and a motive to do it, and no legitimate occasion for the drug, the proof is strong; there is little more needed for a legal, none for a moral conviction.—This is where we now find Gay; he could have done the deed; he was capable of it; a cunning, subtle instrument, well adapted to have accomplished it; and which is useless for any other purpose, is found in his possession. And you will bear in mind that it is not only Phelps and Lake, but also Clark and Van Arman, who prove Gay had a match. This is enough; but over and beyond it, you have the direct admission of Gay, made to the same witnesses. But you are told Gay was such a liar you could not believe him, even when he spoke the truth. You are told Gay is one of the witnesses for the prosecution. There is no attempt to explain how the *principal felon* is a witness for the prosecution. The defence give it to us as an axiom to be received, that Gay is a witness for the prosecution, and he is not to be believed. Gentlemen, I have heard some strong impeachments, as I have been through this cause, I need not tell you I have heard some very weak ones; but I never heard of a liar so great as not to be believed when he confessed his own crimes. But you are told these admissions should not be in evidence; and counsel with the tone of dignified and expressive indignation, desire that the extraordinary admission of these statements of Gay, may go forth to all the world. Let it be known to all courts and lawyers, every where and in all time to come!

> "He spoke, and awful bends his sable brows,
> Shakes his ambrosial curls, and gives the nod,
> The stamp of fate and sanction of the God;
> High heaven with trembling the dread signal took,
> And all Olympus to the centre shook."

As it has been sent forth thus, with high proclamation, I wish the explanation to follow that *they were received without objection* on the part of the defence. I confess I always had some shakings about these admissions, but they were taken without *objection*, and they were given to the jury, if as nothing else, as a theory; for over three months they have been before you; the prosecution closed their evidence and there was no motion to strike them out; the defence proceeded and closed, and still no motion. If they are there wrongfully whether as evidence or theory, the blame is not with us, and as it is clearly proven that they were made; and as it is manifest they are true, for no criminal, much less an old cunning and hardened one like Gay, confesses to crimes of which he is guiltless, you have only the truth and truth can work no injustice. But gentlemen, the case is equally strong without them. Many of the defendants have confessed the same and I will hereafter show you that these confessions are so proven that you must believe them.

But again, gentlemen, if Gay burned the depot according to the evidence and theory of the prosecution, he must have done it with a match similar to that which was described to him by the defendants. But the counsel tells you a match so made and constructed cannot be made to burn, and this is presented to you as a full and perfect defence in itself. To this important point in the case I now invite your attention. I will treat it fairly, and I feel assured, gentlemen, that a close and candid examination of the evidence pertaining to it, will convince you beyond the question of a doubt that a match so made and constructed will burn and is most fiendishly suited for the felonious purposes for which we allege it has been used by these defendants. I will not ask you too perceive that I hold one match in my right hand, and another in my left. I will not produce to you a pistol and demonstrate that it is intended *to shoot*, not to carry slow trains; I will not load one with cotton and invite you to fire it off; I will not produce a box of lucifer matches; I will not set fire to different pieces of cotton and ask you to look upon the smoke and inhale the odour: all this has been done by the learned counsel who has preceded me, and I am bound to admit, done with a grace and dexterity that might make Herr Alexander tremble for his laurels. I will perform no such experiments for you; they do not suit my taste, I doubt if they suit this place. I doubt if the counsel would have entered on their performance if he did not believe you were deeply impressed with the force of his quotation, "what we hear moves us less than what we see."

But gentlemen, even *it* does not hold good here, you are to be moved by what you hear. You hear the evidence, and if it come from a true and reliable source; you are to be moved by, and decide according to it. Such is your oath and so you will do. I do not, for a moment mean to impute to the distinguished counsel any thing unfair. I am satisfied that he intended to practice no deception upon you; high and honorable as he is, the learned counsel would never abuse the practice, but humble imitators led into error by an illustrious example may seek to deceive the judgment rather than lead it by those rules which the wise and learned have laid down as the safest and surest guides to truth. Gentlemen, you are bound to take the law from the court, because it is a science which it has studied and mastered, but with which you are not supposed to be familiar. So also, upon other matters of science and skill, with which it is true you may be but, with which you are not presumed to be familiar, you are bound to receive the opinion of experts; not draw conclusions from experiments which may, even without intention be made the instruments of error or deception.

I will now *discuss* the evidence upon this head. This course may prove less interesting; but it will better enable us to discharge our duties, and will, in the end, prove more satisfactory. I will first call your attention to the description of the match, in the testimony of Phelps. Speaking of his interview with Filley, at page 125, he says: "He described the match; said it was made of a block containing several holes lengthwise of the block, filled with combustible matter, and small holes in the centre, glazed or varnished, filled with turpentine, and sealed over, so when the fire was communicated through the holes or chimneys from the other end, it would melt the wax, and communicate with the turpentine."

As some question has arisen in relation to this portion of the testimony, and it has been differently stated to you, I will here ask the court to read to you that portion of Phelps' testimony, from his minutes.

[The court read from his minutes, and Mr. Van Dyke resumed.]

I am pleased to find, gentlemen, that the minutes taken by the court agree precisely with what I have read. We have got the description given of the match, and it only remains to inquire if a match made according to it, would burn and operate as we allege. We have shown you, by Dr. Desnoyers, that it would. It is conceded that the block used by Dr. Desnoyers, is identical with the one described to Phelps, and the one used at Niles; it is conceded that the match he prepared would and did burn; it is conceded that his match was made thus: the outer holes were filled with cotton, first steeped in a solution of saltpetre, and then dried—with a paper funnel running down the centre; and the centre and small holes, intended as a reservoir to contain the camphene, were lined with glue—this being done by the simple process of pouring the solution of glue in and out again. But the counsel for the defence tells you this is not according to the description; he objects to the glue and the saltpetre, and says the evidence of Phelps excludes them, and requires varnish and camphene in their stead. The prosecution concedes that a lining with varnish will not prevent the absorption of the camphene placed in the reservoir; and that cotton steeped in camphene will not answer for a slow match. But does the description given by Phelps, limit us to the use of these materials? Most certainly not. First, as to the cotton prepared with saltpetre. Is that a departure? He says, "*combustible matter;*" that is something easily susceptible to fire. Does not cotton prepared in saltpetre conform to this requirement? Is it not "combustible matter?" If cotton steeped in camphene will not burn, *it* is excluded by the description; for Mr. Filley spoke of combustible matter that was tried; that *had* burned; and in the efficacy and certainty of which, he expressed unbounded confidence. The cotton, then, used by Dr. Desnoyers, conforms to the description.

But the counsel says there was a departure in lining with glue. Is this so? Does the description limit us to an experiment excluding glue? I think not gentlemen; in ordinary parlance the language is perfectly applicable to glueing; but if the language was ever so inapplicable, it would not still exclude it. What was the end which Filly said was to be attained by the glazing? you remember it without my referring to it; it was to prevent the camphine being absorbed by the wood; how ridiculous then it is to quibble upon the strict accuracy of Mr. Filley's language; what he meant by glazing or varnishing, and I do not care which word you adopt, was something that prevented the diminution of the camphine by absorption. If varnish being soluble in camphine, will not effect that purpose, then he did not mean varnish. Whether his language quite came up to the standard of scientific accuracy or not, he can settle with the distinguished Senator. He meant something that would effect the purpose, for he said it had been tested. To come within his description we must get something that will answer that purpose—varnish or anything else that falls short of that, falls short of what he described.

We are are not confined even to glue; we have only to show you that there is material by which the result can be obtained, and as Filley says, they did not obtain the result, you would be bound to presume that he used that material. How much stranger it is gentlemen, when we show you that glue, a common, cheap material, found in any house, used in the simplest manner, produces the desired effect. You see then that the match prepared by Dr. Desnoyers was made pursuant to the description given; it could not have been otherwise, for he was handed the testimony, and requested to guide his experiments entirely by it.

And now, gentlemen, let us see if that match would be an instrument well adapted to the purposes for which we charge it has been used. You have seen these matches; they are of rough, unfinished design. Dr. Desnoyers tells you, "All the materials used are common in drug stores in the country." Yet he, an eminent chemist, tells you, "For the purpose of burning, I could make no improvement save to line the tube with metal." All his skill, all the secrets of that science in which he has gained an enviable reputation, he tells you could furnish for the incendiary nothing more certain than this match which you are told by counsel is no more fitted for burning than a lump of ice. Dr. Desnoyers does not give you a hasty, inconsiderate opinion; he gives you the result of careful investigation and experiments, and tells you that for the theory relied on by this prosecution this instrument is perfect. Practical experience has brought it to the highest perfection. Skill and science might essay, but in vain to improve it. He tells you that even the common shoemakers' wax, he found upon exprriment to be the best substance for covering the reservoirs of camphene;—his skill suggested other substances, but this he found the best of all. This match, then, is admirably adapted to produce a fire. Look at the testimony, and you will perceive that it is no less admirably adapted to guard the safety of the felon. It is small, light, easily carried, and easily concealed. Witnesses who were present at some of the experiments describe its operation. Mr. Ledyard says: "After a little all appearance of fire or smoke disappeared, and if I had not been aware of it I would not notice there was any fire. As the fire burned through the tubes there was no smell or sign of fire. One of the holes was covered with wax, and after the fire burned through it melted, and camphene oozed through from the hole upon the shavings. Dr. Desnoyers was present. It was about 45 minutes from the time it was lighted till it burned through and fired the shavings." Mr. Larned says: "Several times we had supposed it had gone out, as there was no smoke at all; at the end of about 50 minutes it burned through to the end." Mr. Webster says: "While it was burning through there was no indication whatever of fire, and we supposed it had gone out, but on feeling found it hot."

Thus, you see, with a fearful instrument like this, the incendiary might go along unnoticed and unsuspected even while it was in his hands and consuming with its slow but certain fire. Mr. Ledyard tells you, "There was no smell or sign of fire." Mr. Larned tells you, "There was no smoke." All tell you there was no indication of fire; and yet in the face of testimony like this from a learned and able chemist and gentlemen of the highest respectability, counsel burns cotton on a table and asks you to view the smoke and inhale the smell. But the counsel says all else granted, "The match will not burn over an hour. Dr. Desnoyers' skill cannot carry him beyond that." Is this the testimony, gentlemen? You will remember that Dr. Desnoyers had but a short time to experiment in. Every person knows that in matters like this, complete success is the result of time and long continued experiments. But what does Dr. Desnoyes tell you? "I think it might be made to burn *three hours*." "I don't see how one could be made to burn forty-eight hours. I think to make one burn nine hours would be a doubtful experiment." "I have not carried my experiments far enough to state how long one might be made to burn."

You perceive, gentlemen, that Dr. Desnoyers has done little more than commence his experiments. He says in another place, "I did not try to make one burn over an hour and fifteen minutes. I did not push my experiments beyond that." And even while you hold in your hands testimony like this—while still fresh in your ears, the counsel tells you the skill of a chemist could not make it burn over an hour and ten minutes. The first objection made by the defence was that the match would not burn at all. That was all we had to meet. That was the extent of the proof required, but in almost his first experiments, Dr. Desnoyers finds that he can, by varying the strength of his solutions, graduate the match to burn at will, from five minutes to over an hour—he sees clearly that he could make it burn three hours; further he has not looked or tried to go. If such results as this attends the first efforts, can you assign the limits of nine, twelve, or twenty hours as inadmissible, by longer tubes or prolonged experiments? Again, gentlemen, you will remember that these defendants are not destitute of chemical science. There is among them a chemist of no mean attainments, Dr. Farnham, who, in other portions of the evidence, we find using his chemical knowledge for the ends of this combination, and experimenting on a composition to be used in blowing up the cars. Who can say how many months he spent in experimenting, befor he brought this match to its present state of perfection? This review of the evidence, gentlemen, must convince you that this ground of defence—"*the match would not burn*"—is utterly unsupported; the evidence answers it beyond all possibility of question. Before passing from this branch of the case, I must call your attention to the remarks of counsel in relation to the match which it was conceded did burn. You were told that this was "an after thought," "a subterfuge," "a studied and deliberate fraud on the part of the prosecution." Do such words drop becomingly from the lips of the distinguished counsel? Does he hope to blind you to the detected and exposed frauds attempted by the defence, by making wanton and utterly unfounded charges against the prosecution? In reference to this point of the case, "a studied and deliberate fraud" was attempted, but by whom? Call back the testimony to your minds, and you will readily answer, *by the defence*. To say so is painful to me—the words rise reluctantly to my lips, but they are true, and charged as the prosecution has been, in studied phrases, I must speak them. Was it not an attempt at fraud to prepare matches from cotton and camphene only? try experiments with them in a private office? bring half a dozen men—not a chemist among them—to swear to you they would not burn? represent that they were made in accordance with the description in evidence and exultingly exclaim and proclaim through the streets, that the pretended match was a farce? Was it not an attempt at fraud in the counsel, to tell you in his argument, that the evidence described the match as made from cotton steeped in camphene, and then dwell on the evidence that such would not burn? Where is the evidence describing the match as made with camphened cotton? Has the counsel referred you to it? Has he has even read it from his abstracts of evidence? Nothing of the kind. Not one solitary witness states anything of the kind. The counsel cannot now refer to it. You cannot find it in your books of evidence. I did expect that he would read some such evidence; that some mistake in his minutes had led him into the error; but there is not even that, he does not refer to a single passage, he does not name a single witness—*there is no such evidence.* Contrast this gentleman with the course of the prosecution. When the question was presented they did not try experimento upan false materials in a private closet, and bring men, who though highly respectable, were not chemists, to swear to the result. They at once went to the most eminent chemist in the State—a man, who even in youth, had stored his mind with the riches of science—handed him the testimony, asked him to ascertain if a match made according to that description would burn as stated, and without another word left him to his researches. They placed him an the stand, that he might explain the materials he used, that you might know if he had used any but the simplest, or which were not embraced in the description given, Was this subterfuge? Was this fraud? Has the prosecution stated to you evidence that does not exist, and then based an argument upon it? Has the prosecution misrepresented or suppressed testimony upon any point? The charge of fraud comes badly from the defence, and will re-act fearfully upon it.

The counsel tells you that the match, if placed in a close box, would be extinguished, and therefore Gay could not have carried it, as stated in a box. Doctor Desnoyers tells you: "If the match was placed in a tight box, the cotton might burn, but it would not set fire to the shavings." I now refer you to Gay's statement to Phelps, p. 10: "Gay reiterated his former story how he managed to fire the old depot. He went in while the hands were at work, went up stairs, and deposited the match in the cupola; placed the fire in the box before he left home, and when he left it, took off the cover."

You see, gentlemen, when we refer to the evidence *as it is*, we find that every point raised by the defense serves but to strengthen the prosecution, and bring forth the inherent evidences of truth contained in almost every sentence. On the very first day of the trial, before any one thought of saying the match would not burn, Phelps tells you that Gay carried the match in a box; but he removed the cover when he left it in the cupola. Three months afterwards, Doct. Desnoyers tells you that Gay might carry it lighted in a box; but if he desired it should fire the shavings when it burned through, he should have the cover removed and the air admitted. This, too, is drawn forth, not upon direct, but cross-examination; and I ask you, gentlemen, if in all your experience you ever witnessed so strong a confirmation of the truthfulness of a witness. In May. Phelps tells you the manner in which Gay fired the depot. Will it be said that he artfully added, "left it with the cover off," to meet this unanticipated defense? If he anticipated the difficulty, he would have avoided it, by leaving out all mention of the box; but he told just what he heard, and well for him he told all he heard. A sudden point is raised by the defense. Science is invoked, and by its light we read that while a portion of the sentence led him into difficulty, the remainder led him forth again. Again, you are shown the match delivered to burn at Niles, and told that the cotton it contains will not burn; there is no saltpetre in it; no trace of glue on the reservoirs. Again, the answer comes forth from the testimony, and brings with it new and striking evidences of its truthfulness. Mr. Clark tells you that when the fire at Niles was extinguished, the match was put in the river, and remained there all night. Now listen to Doct. Desnoyers: "If a match prepared as I prepared those used, was in water all night, it would after, show no sign of the preparation, either in the wood or the cotton; the glue and saltpetre would be extracted by the water." A full answer to the point, and more too, gentlemen; for it shows that the match delivered to burn at Niles, and which held camphene for a night and a day, as proven by Clark and Van Arman, must have been prepared in exactly the same manner as those experimented with by Dr. Desnoyers.

But the counsel says the cotton is not soiled by the water; and if the match was placed in the river all night, being light, it would float away. To these objections, the testimony furnishes me no answer. I will merely suggest that the pure limpid waters of the Niles river, are more adapted for cleansing than soiling; and that when Mr. Clark placed it in the river, intending to resume its possession when entirely extinguished, it is not quite impossible he conld have taken precautions against its floating away.

But the counsel says, although Phelps, Clark and Lake say this Niles match was ignited,and set fire to the shavings, there is no trace of fire on the cotton, or in the tube. Gentlemen, the evidence again answering, speaks also to the truthfulness of Phelps. You will remember that Phelps testified that before he set fire to the match at Niles, he poured two spoonfuls of camphene into it and then applied the match. Doct. Desnoyers says: "If camphene was poured round the touch-hole and fired, it would not show sign of fire in the tube." Camphene in the cotton, would prevent its burning while damp; but the camphene on the outside of the match, would of course blaze and set fire to the shavings in the box; and when they were extinguished, of course the cotton would show no sign of fire, which never communicated to it.

I will engage, at the proper time, gentlemen, to show you that Phelps' testimony must be true, but wish you here to note this. If Phelps was a false witness—if, as charged, the matches were his own fabrication, would he have sworn to you that he set fire to the Niles match, and yet produced it to you without a sign of fire within it? He wanted you to believe that he fired it; he wanted you to believe, that when fired, it would inevitably burn thro' the cotton in the tube; he might easily have singed a part of the cotton, but does not: he produces it to you without a sign of fire, without a word of explanation! Is it not again manifest that Phelps spoke the truth; that he was so *conscious* he did so, that he never even looked to see if the match he produced would corroborate or contradict his story? I am glad the defense were so ingenions about a match "not made according to the description;" for it called in the light of science and the result of experiments, without which, this Niles match would have been a stumbling block; but with which, it has become strong evidence of the truthfulness of Phelps.

But counsel exclaimed, here is the match that was found at Gay's, and which was given to burn the new depot; it has not been in the river, yet *it* wont burn—there is no saltpetre in *it*. I perceive that by the printed report of the testimony, gentlemen, it does not appear that the match found at Gay's, is a different one from that shown to Phelps, Clark and Van Arman, as the one with which he was to burn the new depot. This has doubtless led the counsel into his error. The printed report is in almost every particular perfectly reliable; its accuracy reflects great credit on the establishment that published it;

but the occasional omission of words is almost unavoidable. I find by the minutes reported by counsel for the prosecution, that Phelps stated, on the first day, that the match found at Gay's house, (the one referred to by counsel,) was *not* the same shown him by Gay. As this is important, I will ask the court to read you their minutes.

(The court read from their minutes; and it appeared Phelps testified the match found was different from the one shown him.)

Mr. Van Dyke. You perceive then, gentlemen, that the match found at Gay's, is not the one with which the new depot was to be burned. It was in another connection argued by counsel, that as the match was not found at Gay's on the first search, nor until Phelps insisted on a second and more thorough search, Phelps himself placed it where found. Having the facts, gentlemen, it is for us now to draw the conclusions. As shown you by the counsel, during his experiments, the match found at Gay's, wont burn—the cotton is not prepared. I will, however, ask you to look at *that* match. You perceive that one of the fuse holes is burned to almost three times its original size, by repeated attempts to ignite the cotton; it was in this state when found. What is the inference? To my mind, it is plain, that old Gay was endeavoring to learn the secret, and that this was a match he got made to experiment upon. It is remarkable that although Gay showed the match to Phelps, Lake, Van Arman and Clark, he never told them a word of the material that composed it; he was sure it would burn; it had burned; but he never said a word as to the material of which it was made. When they had his confidence so fully, doubtless if he knew, he would have revealed the manner in which it was made. If Phelps was false, would he not have given the description as from Gay, as well as from Filley? We find Gay then possessed of the knowledge that these matches would burn, but ignorant of the manner of preparing them. Though cunning, he was illiterate. Dr. Desnoyers tells you, "when prepared with saltpetre, the cotton would show no sign of preparation to the eye." To Gay it would seem simple cotton. He was a hardened sinner—he loved crime for its profit, but he loved it for itself, too; any knowledge that could aid crime, was to him "great gain." And is it not almost certain that he would, under the circumstances, try to discover this secret, and experiment on simple, unprepared cotton? There is every thing to indicate this: the match in court was not the one received to burn; yet it is evident, that repeated attempts to fire it have been made. Either this theory, or the theory of the defense that Phelps made and placed it there, is the true one. Test the latter. If Phelps made it, he knew it would not burn; for whoever had it, tried to make it burn. Would Phelps, then, cause it to be found and bring it into court merely to stamp perjury on his testimony? He did not need its finding, to corroborate his testimony; for apart from Lake, Messrs. Van Arman and Clark saw the match at Gay's, and to find this one, was quite unnecessary. Phelps insists on the second search. If honest, this was natural: he would say, "I saw the match—it must be on his premises—a further search will find it." This is conduct consistent with the theory of his truth; but if he made the match, it was certainly taking very extra care to produce, what he knew when produced, would be a flat contradiction to his entire testimony.

I have now gentlemen, answered fully the first distinct defence upon which counsel relied. I hope I have kept my promise of answering it not by sophistry but by a candid examination of the testimony. I feel you must be satisfied that " this distinct defence" is entirely disposed of. Incidentally I have also done much, I trust to show you that Phelps is a truthful witness. If so I ask you to retain it in your minds. As anxious to be as brief as possible, I leave this part of the case and will not again return to it.

Without pausing to recapitulate at length you will perceive gentlemen, that the following points are now established. There was a combination among the defendants to injure the company, to if nessessary for their ends burn the Detroit and other depots and that the Detroit depot was wilfully and maliciously burned by Gay, by means of one of these matches placed in the cupola.

I will now gentlemen call your attention to the " second defence" relied on by the counsel. It is by them insisted that the evidence in this case shows that the matches produced were made by Phelps and Lake. If this were so, while I do not see that it would cosntitute a full defence, I feel that it would be a strong and important point. But whether it would or not, bcomes quite immaterial as I will presently show you. There is nothing in the evidence upon which such an opinion can be based. As I review the argument of counsel on this head you will notice that it is constructed mostly upon inferences from *assumed* positions, which have been already overthrown. Thus he says, if the defendants made the matches, they made them to burn; if Phelps—he made them to deceive; then assumes that they will not burn and hence Phelps must have made them. But you have seen that the matches will burn; and you have seen none; you have seen Phelps, over anxious to make the one at Niles burn—poured Camphene in the fuse hole—did the very thing that would prevent it burning, and afterwards produced the matches with the cotton insinged! thus affording the most coclusive evidence that he was utterly ignorant of their qualities and operation. I need not demonstrate to you how powerfully the argument reacts. Again counsels says: By the evidence we first find the matches in the possession of Phelps, and until the contrary appears the law presumes the possessor the maker. If this were so, still, whenever Phelps has a match he accounts for the possession. You must take all his testimony or none; you cannot retain the portion of the sentence where he says, "I had a match" and reject the concluding portion where he says, "I received it from the defendants to burn the Niles depot." But again gentlemen, the statement of the evidence is incorrect; we do not find a match *first* in the possession of Phelps. The first time we trace the actual sight of a match is on page 129 where Phelps says that towards the end of January, Fitch showed him one in the small room at Filleys—the holes bored but not prepared for burning. This proves the match not in the possession of Phelps but in the possession of Fitch and Filley. Phelps also testifies that he saw the same match afterwards at the Centre; but I pass that by. The next place a match is seen, is at Gays', by Phelps in February, and by Phelps, Clark and Van Arman in April, not in the possession or under the control of Phelps or Lake, but of Gay who says he got it from "*his friends at the Centre.*" The next time a match is seen, is on the 11th April at the Centre when it is taken from the small room in Filleys and given by some of the defendants to Phelps and Lake to burn at Niles; and the next time an unprepared match is found under Gay's side walk—to this I have already adverted at length. Now I have given you all the testimony that exists on this head and what is the result. If you retain Phelps' testimony, the first match is seen in January, in the possession of Fitch and Filley. If you reject the testimony of Phelps and Lake then Clark and Van Arman show the first match in the possession of Gay the principal felon who says he received it from some of the defendants. Gentlemen it is a dangerous thing to base an elaborate argument upon a mistatement of evidence. But again the counsel says it is improbable defendants made them. If defendants made the matches, why have not some of the party confessed? why has not the material and tools for making them been found on some of their premises? and counsel gravely adds, thread, paper, and cotton, are used in the formation of the match, but there is no proof of any of these, not even a leaf of paper having been found in any of their houses. Gentlemen there is no proof of any search for such materials; even if search were made, and successfully, it would add nothing to the strength of the prosecution. What are the entire tools and materials necessary? augurs, a plane, thread, paper, cotton, shoemakers wax, and saltpeter; things found in the house of almost every farmer; every one of which are indispensable to a farmer who mends his wagons and cures his pork. The only place searched was Fitch's house and there the search was in a safe for papers; if it were for any thing else you can readily imagine, that the house and premises of an extensive and wealthy farmer, and a man of considerable public and private business were not destitute of paper, thread, and augurs, and even white wood, when we find that a fence of several hundred feet around his premises is partly made of it. But says the counsel, none of the defendants have confessed; if guilty, among so many some would confess. Gentlemen the prosecution has sought no confession, and even if it had, do the guilty always confess? sometimes they do; but do they always? It would be strange indeed to find them confessing, bound together as they were; associating in prison as they did; the younger and tenderer, constantly under the eye of the more hardened; and with learned counsel giving bold assurance of acxuittal even to the last. So far you perceive gentlemen the second distinct defence amounts to nothing: it fades away before testimony without the aid of argument scarcely needing even explanation. But gentlemen I regret that we have not yet done with this head. Much skill and labor has been expended upon it by counsel, an ingeneous theory with dim and distant views of evidence, has been presented, and it is my duty to follow the counsel through the entire of his argument. He tells you this match smells of state prison; that it was invented there while Phelps was an inmate and he must have learned its principle and knowing how to construct, he *probably made it.* The testimony upon this point is as follows; Phelps 145 says: "Never saw in or about the prison at Jackson, any machine or contrivance for burning buildings. Never had any knowledge of such a thing about the prison; think Mr. Titus told me a convict named Houghton, had made a brass canon, which he wanted him to take to Washington and get patented. Don't know that I ever had any definite description of the machine or canon.

Mr. Titus, the prison agnnt, says: "I remember a revolving cannon being constructed by Houghton; never knew of Phelps or Lake having anything to do with it: Houghton showed me a piece of wood and with his pencil showed me the principle: in looking over a patent report I found the principle had been patented: showed it to Houghton, and it was the last I heard of it."

This is the entire testimony, upon this point, and you see it repels all knowledge on the part of Phelps, of the State Prison invention, even if that invention at all resembled this match which is not shown; and yet on this you are gravely asked to presume that Phelps learned the act of making matches in prison, and continued to practice it when he left. To proceed. The counsel says before any match was seen by others than Phelps and Lake, they borrowed augers from Metcalf, which correspond with the size of the bores in the match; that upon their being borrowed Phelps takes his wife to Niles, leaving Lake alone in his house—that Metcalf called at the house, found Lake with closed doors; when he knocked, the door was only partially opened. Lake answered an inquiry and closed it again; that Cowdon also called, found Lake with closed doors, and working with saws, augers, planes and shavings, &c.—evidently making matches. Such gentlemen, as near as my memory serves is an outline of the imposing syoposis given of the testimony. I must again read you the testimony at some length, as I am sure the full testimony will be more satisfactory to you. There seems fearful secrecy in Phelps taking away his wife—not even she could be there; Lake must be left perfectly alone in the house. *You* will remember however, Phelps was going to Niles and his wife had a relation there whom she went to visit: but Lake was alone in the house with closed doors. This is explained by Mr. Phelps, who says: "The fastening to our door was a latch and thumb piece, which often fell out if the door was shut hard." And again, on cross examination, "when the thumb piece fell it fell outside." Nothing very wonderful then, in the fact that Mr. Metcalf found the door closed and Lake inside; but the counsel would have you believe that he half opened the door and was unwilling Metcalf should come in. Here is the testimony of Mr. Metcalf, an honest man, and I ask you does it convey any such impression? On direct examination he says: "Went to his house once to see Phelps in the spring: the thumb piece was out, and I knocked. Lake came tothe door, and told me that Phelps had gone to his father's, and I followed and overtook Phelps, and did my business with him."

On cross examination: "The day the thumb piece was gone, Lake came to the door and told me Phelps must be almost half way to the old gent.'s and I hallowed after Phelps. Lake opened the door about a foot—enough to put his head well out—I didn't ask or want to go in."

His business was to see Phelps. Phelps was then passing out of sight, and there was no great secrecy surely in Lake not insisting on Metcalf's entering when he dind'nt want to go in. But how account for borrowing the augers? Phelps, Lake and Mrs. Phelps all say the augers were borrowed to mend the buggy and returned the same morning—that old Mr. Metcalf himself took them back. Mrs. Phelps says: "I remember the wagon being broken, and Phelps sending Lake to Metcalf's to borrow augers to mend it; the springs were broken and he bored holes and tied it up; we went to Niles that day; Metcalf came there the same day and took the augers home; Phelps told him we were going away, and to take them home."

Now let us examine if there was great secrecy in the manner of getting the two augers. Was it designed or mere accident? Lake when recalled on the 30th of August, says: "Phelps once sent me and I borrowed some augers from Metcalf to mend his buggy. I told M. I did not know what size he wanted and he told me to take two or three—brought them to Phelps, he used them to mend the buggy—they were used for no other purpose. Am strongly of the impression that Metcalf took them home the same day."

Mr. Metcalf says: "I don't know how many augers I had at the time: I don't recollect that L. did not at first know which auger to take, but I may have said to him to take more."

Mr. Metcalf evidently remembers little beyond the mere fact that the augers were borrowed. At one time he thinks they were borrowed beforethe day he knocked at the door he tells you frankly that he may have said to Lake to "take two instead of one;" also, that, "he don't know if the augers were returned the same day they were borrowed." And yet, you are told this negative testimony—this I don't know—of Metcalf, must outweigh the affirmative testimony of these witnesses. We have still the testimony of General Heber Cowden; the gentleman who gets divorces without a witness, who saw Lake through a window on the north side of the house where you observe there was none, who saw Lake writing at a bureau, while Mr. Phelps and Mrs. Metcalf tell you there was no bureau there; and who saw the shavings, the augers, the baskets, the wood, almost the matches themselves. Far be it trom me to impute the least want of truth to the General. The brave are always truthful. He saw Lake through the side of a house where there was no window or crevice, and at a bureau when there was none. *Scarcely credible.* He saw planes augers and shavings, I will show that is scarcely credible. But the General is one of the keen sighted, described by Hudibras:

"He must have optics sharp, I ween,
Who sees what is not to be seen."

He does not tally with the other facts and the theory of the defence. It was so necessary that Lake should be perfectly alone, that Phelps carries off his wife and child to Niles, and yet Lake carries on the deep mystery so unguardedly that every wandering vagrant who may happen to be strolling through the country, and every man who may wish to see Phelps at his house, has only to fling a peeping glance at the window as he goes by, and lo! the dread secret is discovered. You cannot forget the manner of this witness on the stand. His affected frankness, and yet his evident leaning for certain of the defendants; his unqualified certainty that there was a window on the north side of the house, through which he saw; his subsequent uncertainty of the same day: afterwards, his apparent confusion and manifest contradictions, would almost justify a suspicion that there were more here in the plot to charge these matches on to Phelps; then the tamarack witness from Indiana.

What a farce! all this secresy ends in this; the first stranger who comes along is freely, admitted to see the entire. Cowden says Lake informed him Phelps had gone to Niles, and the solution of all the General's blunders, is that he called the same day, while every thing was in confusion, and Lake himself preparing to depart; the disorder of the house shocked his military precision and confused his ideas and led him into a fourth error. Is not this a charitable if not the true solution? Lake, when last on the stand, tells you the day Phelps went to Niles, he left for Whittemore Lake, taking Phelps' horse and buggy with him and stayed until the day Phelps arranged to be home, some five or six days after. If this is true, it is absurd to prove that the augers were borrowed to make matches at Phelps, when there was no one there to use them. If untrue, how susceptible of disproof, for it would be impossible for Lake to have remained in the house and kept the horse and buggy during Phelps' absence, without the knowledge of the neighbors. The people at Whittemore Lake were also accessible, yet no attempt is made to disprove the truth of the statement that all the time Phelps was at Niles, Lake was at Whittemore Lake. The sum total, then, is this, there was no secresy, but sometimes the thumb-piece fell out; augers were borrowed, but to mend a buggy. If what has been said is not enough then I will ask you to look at the match and the augers, and as many of you are skilled in such matters, you will at once perceive that these old augers never could have bored the holes in the match: though the same size, they are old and worn and never could have been madato bore these holes. It would have required a different instrument—what is generally I believe, called a bit, to have effected the purpose.

But there was a piece of white wood, found by Fenn under the hay in Phelps' hovel. Whether a match could be made from it or not you can judge, and this was a portion of the inanimate nature, which was to speak so loud. I venture to believe you are satisfied the matches never came from it. The concentric rings won't agree. You have, by consent of parties, examined it for yourselves; but as to how it came in the manger I have a word to say. Fenn and Lappin went there at the request of one of the defendants, Burnett. They admit that, when he sent them, he seemed satisfied their toil would not be all in vain—with every assurance he gave the command, "search and ye shall find." Strange, too, these searchers go straight to the hovel and call for a fork. Stranger still, as Mr. Moses Metcalf tells us, he is a witness for the defence:

"*They seemed strongly impressed they would find somhthing.* When he got the fork F. went right to the manger and in a few minutes found the timber. As soon as the fork struck, he said to the Dr., I *guess we have found it,* and he drew it out. I did not see what it was, when he spoke. I guess he did not search much after."

No, they thus find a piece of porous dry whitewood, which they say had lain, at least, three months in the wet yet heated hay—and still there is not a stain of a hairs thickness on it. Now, gentlemen, adopt for the moment the hypothesis that the defendants, or some officious friend, like Parson Billings, had placed it there—is not this precisely the manner in which it would be found? There would be a certainty felt that they would find. There would be an accurate knowledge of the spot to find in, and an assurance, when the fork struck, before even the hay was removed, that, "they had found it." Truly, gentlemen, "who hides finds." But Fenn and Lappin say they did not go direct to the hovel—they first examined carefully the threshing machine in the woods, while Alfred Metcalf was geting a fork—but, unfortunately, this does not agree with Metcalf, who says he went to get the fork and his father:

"My father was about sixteen rods off, but I did not go all the way to him. When I left I left them in the stable—perhaps I was away two or three minutes. While I was on the other side of the house I was out of sight of the stable.This was for part of the two or three minutes. I did not see them go to the woods. When I returned I supposed they were in the stable. I was two or four minutes gone. I went about eight rods and back. The threshing machine is about ten rods from the stable. They had not to my knowledge searched any place before turning out the hay."

Now, gentlemen, having seen that the manner of finding the block raises the idea that the block was placed there by some one at the instance of defendants—I will ask you if other facts, proven, do not repel the idea that it was placed there by Phelps? If he put it there it was to conceal it—yet goes off and leaves it to be discovered by the next occupant. But, not content with this imprudence, he takes measures to insure its being found, for Wm. Reynolds, a witness called to impeach Phelps, says:

"When he left Metcalf's he gave me some hay he left in the hovel—he came to me and told me I might have it. He so told me in April last."

You have no direct proof who placed the stick there. You are, from other facts, to infer whether it is more probable that Phelps or the defendants placed it there. You have the facts and I leave you to draw the inference—regretting, however, that you have been denied the evidence of Cooper, which would so materially aid you.

In relation to cattle guards much has been said. I do not feel at liberty to trespass on your time by discussing a matter that the evidence has made so plain. The defence introduced many witnesses to prove that a cattle guard was broken and left at a crossing near Phelps' house, some of whom said that the block in question might be a portion of it; but H. H. Bingham and Wm. Wycoff, whose testimony you will remember, and who had charge of that portion of the road and passed over it twice a day, prove these witnesses must have been missaken, that there was no broken guard left there, that the only broken guard for miles along there, was one at another place, given to and taken away by another person. One word as to the testimony of Stow. He states that on the evening of the tenth of April Phelps went to the hovel and he, from the gate on the roadside; saw him through an opening in the side of the building bending over the manger. The design of this proof is manifest—it is to imply that Phelps had the Niles match concealed there and went to take it away. Whether this witness is mistaken or has sworn falsely is a matter of indifference to the prosecution; that this testimony is not true, is obvious. That Phelps, after he left the premises and another occupant had entered, would conceal a match iu the manger of an open hovel, is too absurd to impose on the most credulous. And, in addition to this, their own witness, Alfred Metcalf, proves that, at the time stated by Stow, that opening was covered by a buggy shed, which would, of course, prevent the possibility of Stow seeing as stated. It is on a par with General Cowden seeing through the side of a house.

I have now, gentlemen, reviewed the "second perfect defence." You see what it amounts to—that there is not a scintilla of evidence to sustain it—that it has literally no foundation in the case. For anything that appears in evidence there is just as much probability that you made the match as that Phelps made it. One word, in reference to Lake, and then I leave this " second defence" to your consideration. The learned counsel has, all through this branch of his argument, spoken of Lake as an "engineer," "a cunning worker in wood." You will not be misled by these terms. There is no evidence that Lake is either an engineer or worker in wood. Gentlemen, as the testimony of the witness, Henry Phelps, is closely interwoven with such portions of the case as yet remain to be to considered, and inasmuch as the chief strength of the defence has been put forth to impair it, it is proper that I should now advert to him, his position before you and the grounds upon which you are required to withhold credence from him—for you will not have failed to, perceive that, before asking you to rely on the testimoy of any witness I have shown you that he was unassailed or that though assailed, he was still entitled to be believed.

You have listened to the bitter, I will not say fiendish, tirade which counsel have deemed it expedient to indulge in against this witness I concede to the advocate the duty of probing to the quick the tale he deems false, and the motive he thinks corrupt. I concede the necessity of his laying bare to the gaze of the jury and the world, the weakness of the evidence, and the mistakes or perjury of the witness. And when founded in fairness and justice, the earnest and truthful exposure will make the lieing witness to tremble and shrink before the indignant voice of justice. But if counsel deem it their privilege to wander from the truth—to conjure up from bilious fancy, or gather from malignant foes, details of crime not in evidence, in the hope of blasting the reputation and wounding the feelings of a witness; if they suppose, that blessed with wealth and honor; standing in pride of place—"the glass of fashion and the mould of form," it is within their province to trample on the humble—point the finger of derision at his poverty—ridicule the features his Maker has given him—and as if all this would not make his flesh quiver enough, tell him of his dead children in the presence of their living mother, then the counsel who have done all this, and more, stand justified before you. But if fair men turn with distaste from rank injustice—if they discover that the picture is the mere offspring of excited hate, and shrink from its deformities, let not the artists complain of the reaction, or affect surprise at the scorn which consigns their master-piece to fester in unenvied notoriety.

I declare to you, gentlemen, that the biography presented by the counsel who last addressed you, of the witness Phelps, is unwarranted by the facts before you, and discolored all over by the spirit and breath of calumny. I dislike to have to say that the assertions of counsel are untrue; yet I must negate them when not sustained by testimony. Time does not suffice to state them upon this head at length or in number; but I submit to you that no more garbled and unfair representation has ever been made from testimony, than in this particular. It is *not* true that "Phelps went to Michigan Centre and bought a distillery and its stock, with drafts on a person who never could be found." It is *not* true that after removing to Milford, "his stock of goods was suddenly and mysteriously surrendered to the merchants at Buffalo." It is *not* true that his affidavits were questioned; his art in conducting trials questioned, or that "his reputation waned." But why follow out this miserable policy of trying to mislead an intelligent jury by infusing unwarranted prejudices, instead of convincing their judgment by truth and reason. The facts are, so far as we know from the evidence, that Phelps was born of decent parents; received an ordinary education; and came to Michigan, in early life, with an unblemished name; that kindly manners, fair ability and good habits, gained him friends and influence; that his energy, activity, and kind of business, did sometimes bring him into collision with others, and woke up unkindly feelings; but that, until the unfortunate event which led to his conviction of crime, there is no good cause shown for us to believe that his name had become blighted, or his character for truth suspected.

He was charged with larceny. He protested his innocence. He was tried, condemned, and sentenced. Through all the long endurance of his imprisoned years, he yielded respectfully to discipline;

gained the good will of his superiors; still averred his entire innocence; and finally, on an investigation of his case, was freely pardoned by the appropriate power.

If he sinned, most grievously did he expiate it. For years, he was shut out from the green earth, from society, from home and wife and child; from all that makes life desirable, to suffer amid gloom and sorrow.

But the hour of grace came at last; one daylight streak broke from the long dark night, and the ransomed prisoner came forth, once more to look out on this beauteous earth. He turned to no haunted recesses of vice; he joined no wicked band; he participated in no licentious revels. He hastened, rapid as weary limb would bear him, to wife and child. He arrived at the door of his long lost home, travel-stained and worn, and oh! how must the weary pilgrim have felt as the blessed sight grew visible before his ardent vision; the threshhold was crossed; his wife was in his arms; the bitter memory of infamy, the dark sorrows and sufferings of years were lost and vanished in hallowed joy, renewed hope, and united affection.

God's benison on the true woman, who, amid the scoffs of the world—amid its bitterest visitations and severest fates—amid absence and all that tries the soul and wrinkles the brow, proves true to the husband of her better years. Nor can I believe that he who excited such affection—who thus hastened to a virtuous home—and who for years afterwards remained true to it, can be all evil.

As for Henry Phelps, I will show you shortly that he is uncontradicted in any material respect; that he is not successfully impeached—that he is well sustained—that his story is natural, truthful, corroborated and marked all over with the evidences of inherent truth. For the present I beg to submit to you in all candor, that the attack upon his life, his family, his features and affections, is one of those bad mistakes which seldom emanate from any but a desperate and bad defence.

You are told that Phelps is not to be believed because he is impeached. Is he impeached? One hundred and twenty-four witnesses were placed upon the stand, for the purpose of impeaching him, but *did* their evidence amount to an impeachment? I will ask the court to charge you, and I have no doubt they will charge you that impeachment cannot be based upon the knowledge of the impeaching witnesses as to any distinct untruth—nor upon any particular transactions—nor upon character and reputation for anything bnt truth and veracity—that the reputation of the man impeached must be so notorious as to be the general belief of his neighbors and associates. Anything short of this falls short of impeachment. One hundred and twenty-four witnesses were sworn to this point; it would be an endless task—an unpardonable trespass on your time to attempt to review their testimony. I do not believe that the case requires it—but I ask you gentlemen to recall the impression made upon your minds during the examination of these witnesses. I ask you in all candor, if in the entire one hundred and twenty-four, there were a dozen exceptions to the rule, that each examination was a farce. One witness impeached him because he believed he feigned sickness to avoid labor; another because his heart told him not to believe a man who had been in State Prison; another, because he had for ten years judged character by the face—he was a practicle physiognomist, and Phelps' countenance strikes him unfavorably. Were not these things so? Did you not feel during its continuance that the impeachment was ridiculous? If you felt so then when the testimony was fresh and clear in your minds—when the manner and demeanor of each witness was before you, why not feel so now? Nothing has occurred to give to the impeachment a valadity that it did not then possess. I will however present to you a table of those witnesses; I will not call it a perfectly impartial one, because it is not—it is made more favorable to the impeachment than to the prosecution. You will remember that Phelps was over four years in State Prison—he was pardoned—went to the neighborhood of Sylvan and Sharon and resided there for over two years prior to the commencement of these proceeding—although he went to prison wrongfully, although he was pardoned on the ground of wrongful conviction—still he was from prison—suspicions would hang darkly around him—apparent deviations from truth and probity which would pass unheeded in others, in him would swell into grave indications of depravity;—his was not the task of *preserving* a good reputation—he had to make one in the teeth of general prejudice. If, under such circumstances his truthfulness remained unquestioned for two years by the generality of his neighbors, you will admit he did much—that his walk in life must have been correct—that his character for truth must have been good. If there were during those two years but five men who had intimated ought against his truth, it would have run like wild fire through that community—man, woman and child would have heard it. The Court will, I have no doubt, instruct you that character spoken of since the commencement of this trial and growing out of his evidence in it, is to be disregarded,— a wise rule which prevents the perversion of justice by creating false reputation to destroy the testimony of witnesses.

Now gentlemen, out of the 124 witnesses, the learned counsel admits there are but 27 who speak of his reputation since coming from prison, and before these arrests: by every rule of law and by every rule of sense, this is no impeachment—out of an entire neighborhood every man in which all seem willing to hound this witness on to infamy—124 of the most available are selected, and only 27 pretend that during these two years, his truth was ever questioned. They have brought all they could—every living man—from the man who would impeach for feigning sickness down to the man who impeached upon view of faces—every one that could breathe a word against Phelps, was here—townships and counties were ransacked, 124 were all who could be found willing to say a word against him, and of these only twenty-seven could come to the point. Gentlemen, I ask you can twenty-seven men under the circumstances in which they testify make a reputation,—is character so light a thing that it can thus be blown away? The counsel felt that his impeachment was a failure;

that it was not a legal impeachment, and although a lawyer he told you that the rest proved he was guilty or suspected of stealing wheat, horses, &c. &c., and forgetting that you were sworn to go by legal rules, claimed that these illegally formed opiniohs should weigh with you. Gentlemen, one word, as to the reason and wisdom of the rule you are asked to disregard. If it were allowed to impeach a witness because he was suspected or charged with offences—justice would require that he should be permitted to show the charges and suspicions unfounded; and in each case jurors would have to try not one, but one thousand issues; the wheels of justice would be clogged; causes could never be tried, or else all other business should be abandoned—the whole community being necessary to dispose of them. You see the wisdom and necessity of the rule. Now let us look to the fairness and justice of the counsel's request, that in this case you should give weight to the witnesses who impeached Phelps and on cross examination, showed they did so because he was accused or suspected of offences. You will find that six of the witnesses based their impeachment solely on rumors that Phelps stole Orman Clark's horses—twelve others entirely on rumors that he stole Butterfield's wheat—six others on the fact that he travelled from place to place without knowing of any particular business he had for so doing—three upon rumor that he pretended to own land in Oakland County, and eight on rumor that he falsely pretended to have money to lend; there are plenty others of the same character, but these are enough to illustrate by. The prosecution stood prepared to prove these rumors unfounded—to prove Phelps stole neither horses or wheat—that he had land in Oakland county, &c. &c. On the 11th August we placed Mr. Orman Clark on the stand' and asked him if Phelps had stolen his horses, or if he ever suspected or accused him of it. Was the question put? No! Mr. Seward the counsel for the defendants who urged you to consider that if their witnesses failed to impeach Phelps for truth and veracity—they at least had shown you that he was suspected of stealing horses, and that ought to do against his credit—this same identical and learned counsel objected, and the Court very properly held—that it was "true Drew (an impeaching witness) stated so, but as it was immaterial and not propper grounds to form an opinion as to truth, the testimony cannot be received. The testimony of Drew on this point being immaterial and irrelevant."

You willl admit, then gentlemen, that there is candor and fairness in asking you to weigh against Phelps' truth, the proof that he stole horses! Shall I proceed with the investigation of this impeaching testimony? I do not believe it is necessary. If you think it is worth explaining, you will find that the 27—the choice spirits who came up to the sticking Point, in almost every instance, admit disputes with Phelps and show themselves his bitter enemies. Get the 27, and it will recall the words so often sung in your ears—"Godfrey told me;" "Stevenson told me." You will also remember that not a witness could state a single offence or immoral act done by Phelps since leaving prison; here we had over one hundred of his neighbors, selected as the ones who hated him, who would blast his reputation and place the brand of liar on his forehead if they dare; yet not one of them ever knew of his doing an illegal act or even an immoral one. A. says B. told him he heard and B. says A. told him back again, but not one says I knew he did it, and the witness who is on the stand to day "I knew he did not do it" is prevented by the counsel. Gentlemen, if the prosecution insisted upon the strict rule of law, not 20 of these 124 witnesses could have testified at all. But Phelps was a stranger to us; the defence said he was a bad man. If he was such we wished you should know it; he was an important witness in an important cause, and we wished that you should see him as he was. In your hearing we told the defence that we would not hedge them even by legal rules; that in this instance, we would waive our rights, throw down the barriers, and let them follow Phelps' reputation at all times, and in all places, to the fullest extent; they availed themselves of the permission. Their witnesses proved to you that it was *rumored* he stole horses; then they put up the bars (it was their *legal* right to do so) and we could not prove the rumor false. Yet they tell you that the prosecution has been harsh and oppressive.

One word gentlemen as to the witnesses who sustain Phelps the counsel stated them at 118 they are only 101. You are told they amount to nothing. I will not trespass on your time, in reference to them; most of them are men known to you; all of them are men of standing and respectability; you are told they admit that they know nothing of his reputation. This is extracted from the expression they all use that they never heard his truth questioned; the best evidence that it was good. Is there one among them who was not acquainted with Phelps' neighbors or associates? Is there one among them who does not tell you that from acquaintance with the neighbors and associates of Phelps, and the people he did business with, they would know if his reputation was bad? Not one, such was the first question put; unless answered in the affirmative they could not testify, and you will remember that others were called, but the prosecution declined to examine those who said they knew Phelps' associates but slightly; none were examined but those who could say they had means of information; men like Nathan Pierce who said he knew his neighbors; he had seen him at justice courts, heard him sworn as a witness, but never heard his truth questioned; like the Rev, Mr. Moulton, who says: "I am acquainted thro' the whole township;" like Wines who says: "I am well acquainted with the people in the Metcalf neighborhood;" like Sutherland who says he "did work for Phelps, and before giving credit, &c. inquired among his neighbors if he was a man who would do as he agreed &c.;" like Wm. Sprague who gave him a Captains commission but before doing so inquired as to his character, and says: "My object was to find if he could be relied upon as to statements he would make, and if he was suitable for the commsision;" like Rev. Mr. Madison who says: "I was among those who knew P. and heard him frequently spoken of, had an opportunity of knowing his reputation there, never heard anything against his truth, would believe him, &c;" like Mallon Wines who says: "I knew P. in Sylvan, and knew most of his neighbors, well known through the town, sometimes thought I knew every man in the town, supposed his reputation for truth good, never heard it questioned till those arrests, would believe, &c."

I will not proceed—you will remember, gentlemen, that these are not selections, but fair specimens of the 101 witnesses whom, I am told, knew nothing of Phelps, and whose evidence is worthless. The counsel dwelt upon his reputation in prison, but you heard Mr. Titus, the agent, testify he was one of the most reliable men there. You heard Dr. Mowrey say he was on a prison committee, and inquired as to Phelps' character and conduct there, and found it s good he joined in the effort to procure his pardon. Before leaving this branch of the case, justice to the absent requires I should call your attention to one remark of the counsel—it may also serve to illustrate the fairness and candor with which he treats testimony. He told you, alluding to the sustaining witnesses, that (I use his very words):

"One, Samuel Chadwick, says that he himself took his neighbor's watch clandestinely, and wore it until it was advertised and then delivered it up and demanded ten dollars, upon the false pretence that he had paid that money to reclaim it."

A serious charge to make against a witness, a fearful one if it is falsely made, and against an honest man. The testimony of Mr. Chadwick, upon which this charge is made, is:

"Mr. Merriman lost a watch in Jackson. I took it as a matter of joke between him and me, and came to Detroit for two or three days; when I returned I gave the watch to him. I did not tell him how I got it. I told him a man in Detroit gave it to me. Don't remember telling him I gave, or that the man in Detroit wanted $10 for it. Don't recollect telling him so, but won't swear I did not. He did not give me ten dollars. I didn't get the watch from a man in Detroit.

I am very intimate with Merriman and others, and it is common for us to take each other's kerchiefs and things for joke. It was thus I took the watch. I intended returning it at once, but business called me suddenly to Detroit, and while I was away he offered a reward, and when I returned I went to his store and gave it to him, saying a negro in Detroit gave it to me. He is now my family physician, and we continue on good terms. I took it merely as a joke. Others have taken things from in a similar manner and returned them."

I regret to detain you reading this testimony; but charaeter is a precious jewel. It was due to Mr. Chadwick, that as you heard the charge, you should hear the basis upon which it was made. I leave it to you to judge whether the counsel acted well or wisely in making this charge.

I have now done with the impeachment. I feel that as you consider the testimony on both sides of this question, you will come to the same conclusion that I have—that the character of the witness rises from it, not weakened but strengthened. How few characters could have passed through such an ordeal, and come forth so slightly impaired. For weeks, agents have been scouring the country; whole families and neighborhoods have been brought here; the man who could say a word against Phelps—who could breath a suspicion on his fame, stood at a premium. No cost or effort was spared to procure him. And the result is, 27 enemies come upon the stand and say, from what they have heard, mostly each from the other, they would not believe him; 93 other enemies swear they would not believe him, but have no receivable reason for so saying; and 100 good and reliable citizens—men who know Phelps, and know what has generally been said of him, say they would believe him; his truth has never been questioned. I thank the gentlemen for entering on this field of inqutry; it has established the truthful character of Phelps; it has shown it so strong that ingenuity, activity, diligence, industry, perseverance, money, all united, could not destroy it.

But the counsel tells you if Phelps is not impeached, still you are not to believe him, for he is contradicted in several material points. It now becomes my duty, gentlemen, to show you that Phelps is not successfully contradicted in a single material point. I believe gentlemen, that I can show you by fair investigation of the testimony that he is not contradicted on *any* point. I feel certain that not I, but the evidence will convince you that despite the extraordinary and desperate means resorted to, he remains entirely uncontradicted or abundantly sustained as to every material thing he has testified to. It is my intention gentlemen, to take up and discuss every single contradiction of Phelps, which is alleged to exist. I will not take merely those which are most easily answered. I will refer to them all. I will show that in such as are material, he is altogether uncontradicted, or that there are such inherent evidences or corroborations of his truth that you cannot choose but believe him.

1. The learned counsel tells you that Phelps says he met Fitch in Jackson the day before Christmas, and at his request went the next (Christmas) day to the Centre; but that other witnesses prove clearly that Fitch was not in Jackson the day before Christmas. We admit that this is proven, but still there is no contradiction of Phelps; simply because Phelps does not swear as counsel says he does, and the contradiction springs not from evidence, but from a (perhaps unintentional) misrepresentation of it. I do not ask you to take my word for this, though I do trust that the candor I have heretofore evinced, would entitle it to some weight. I refer you to the testimony of Phelps p. 125, which says:

"Saw him (Fitch) next in about a week, on a Monday at Jackson, in front of Holden's hat store; had but little talk there. He told me the "boys" were going to be at the Centre the next day, and I had better be there; think he said he could'nt be there himself; told him I would go down, and did go." Again at p. 160, he says:

"I cannot say whether it was the Monday before or the day before Christmas; can't say positively what day Christmas came on, but think it was Wednesday; am sure it was Monday I saw Fitch, and that I went to the Centre, Christmas; but I don't know if Christmas was on Tuesday or Wednesday."

A reference to an almanac will show you that Chistmas day was Wednesday, so that instead of swearing he saw him the day before Christmas, the witness swears he saw him the day *but one* before Christmas, and swears further that Fitch then told him he was to be from home on Christmas day, a fact subsequently proven. *Contradictions(?)* like this, solemnly announced, must react fearfully upon the defence. This *one* is a strong corroboration. How could Phelps know Fitch was to be from home on Christmas day? Phelps tells you he made written reports after each interview, to the agents of the Company. Why did they not call for the report of that interview, and see if he reported the Monday before Christmas that Fitch was to be from home; why did they not even ask to see the diary he had in court, and in which he said every particular was entered as it occurred?

2. The counsel says that Phelps testifies to Willard Champlin's having gone to G. Filleys, and there made certain admissions; and that Hart Holmes proves that Champlin did not go to G. Filleys on that occasion. But, gentlemen, by referring to the testimony of Phelps, p. 130, you will perceive he speaks of an occurrence about the time he came to Detroit. (12th February.) Turn to Hart Holmes' testimony, and you find that he speaks of a period in March; again the time Phelps speaks of, they went to avoid some persons looking for stolen property; but turn to Hart Holmes, and you find he speaks of an occasion when they went to a ball. This contradiction then vanishes, not before sophistry, but before the reading of the testimony.

3. The counsel says that Phelps could not have had the interviews he states with Fitch on the day of the 12th at the depot on his arrival and on the next day, when they spoke about fish. In reference to the first interview, they rely on Holden, whose testimony I have already referred to in connection with Wescott. You will remember that Holden merely says that after he got his valise he went to tne hotel across the street and thinks he saw Fitch immediately after getting into the hotel. There is no evidence of how long he took, amid the crowd and hurry of the passengers, in getting his valise, or how long he may have been in the hotel before meeting Fitch—while, on the other hand, Wescott and Mr. Doane, p. 121, prove that Fitch was at the depot the night Phelps got in, that he said he was waiting for some person, and that after the arrival of the cars they saw him speaking with some person. Doane says he cannot tell if it was Phelps, as he does not know Phelps. There is no doubt, then, of this interview; and though the counsel says the person he was waiting for was I. R. Brown, there is no evidence of it. On the contrary, there is conclusive presumption against it, for on the 17th July the defence swore I. R. Brown to another point, but never asked him if he came to Detroit in February. Never asked him if he had agreed to meet Fitch here. If the fact counsel states to you is true—if Mr. Fitch was thus waiting for Brown—Brown came on the stand, and why did not they prove it?—In reference to the second interview, Phelps—p. 131—says:

(Here counsel read the testimony.)

And Mr. Sheeley, at p. 157, says.

(Here counsel read the testimony of Mr. Sheeley.)

I now ask you, gentlemen, if in all your experience you ever knew of a stronger corroboration? Is it a got up corroboration? Mark the words of Mr, Sheeley. After testifying, as I have read to the same conversation as Phelps—"I left them talking, and heard this conversation as I passed them; I never told of this or thought of it afterwards, until Phelps appeared before the grand jury, which brought the subject to my memory; I was a member of the grand jury; I think the shabby dressed man had his pantaloons in the tops of his boots; wore a cap, and I think had an overcoat."

The conversation about fish might be trivial—if so, it only shows that Phelps tells all—not merely what he deems important, but all even down to the lightest minutiæ—a feature that always characterises the evidence of a truthful witness, but is never seen in that of a false one. Truth is not easily impeached. We find that while Phelps by the fulness of his details exposes himself to numberless contradictions, instead of contradictions, corroborations spring up around every line of his testimony. They come even from the grand Jury room.

The counsel in his argument relied on the testimony of the other Mr. Brown that at or near the same place he also asked Mr. Fitch about fish, and implying that this was the conversation Mr. Sheeley heard. I was somewhat surprised at this; doubtless, gentlemen, you also were, for apart from the fact that Mr. Sheeley recognised both Fitch and Phelps you will remember Mr. Howard for the defence stopped the further examination of Mr. Brown by saying they did not claim that to be the conversation alluded to by Mr. Sheeley.

But the counsel tells you Fitch came to Detroit on business for Mr. Collier, and truly Mr. Collier did prove that; but yet there is something so remarkable in the evidence of Mr. Collier that I must ask you to listen to it. He says: "I did employ him to come to Detroit. I set no time for his coming, but he said he would come in one or two weeks. I wished him to come to make some investigation as to the origin of the fire in the depot at Detroit, and to see persons employed from his neighborhood who were in the employ of the company, among others Josiah Wells and Caswell, and others were mentioned whom he said he was acquainted with it, and who were at work for the company. My object was, I wished to recover from the railroad company pay for goods burned in the depot. I had goods burned in the depot. When I left home I had no idea of employing Fitch, but after I saw him I concluded to employ him. I left home with the intention of seeing Fitch on that business, and for no other purpose. When I left home I did not intend employing Fitch. I never met him before that time."

If the prosecution had known of this testimony, they would certainly have introduced it. It strongly corroborates the entire theory of the prosecution. How came Mr. Collier, an entire stranger, to go and consult Fitch about the fire? After he saw him, how came he to send him here to investigate? Was a "country gentleman," living seventy miles from Detroit, the person likely to be employed on such business by a stranger? No. But when Collier saw him and learned his intimacy with Wells and Caswell, employees of the company, he employed him. You will remember that the defence has all through disclaimed any particular intimacy between Wells, Caswell and Fitch; yet from their own witnesses we find Fitch procuring employment, to bring him around the depot, upon the ground of his intimacy and influence with them. How perfectly this evidence harmonizes with Phelps' testimony. If it is true, how natural it would be for Fitch to seek some business that would give him a legitimate excuse to see these persons and go about the depot? If it is untrue, how improbable it seems that Fitch would *seek* such employment, yet he did seek it, for till Collier saw him, he had no idea of employing Fitch. I do not claim that this is "conclusive," but I do claim, gentlemen, that the testimony of their own witness is more consistent with the theory of the prosecution than any of the many theories of the defence.

4. The counsel tells you Phelps says a certain conversation between himself, Corwin, Freeland, and Williams, at Coykendall's was interrupted by High saying, "boys what's the privacy?" High proves that he has no recollection of it. Stid also says *he did not see* Phelps at Leoni on the day of a horse trade, which is said to be the day referred to by Phelps, and so far there *seems* to be a contradiction. But is there such? If the thing is untrue how grossly improbable that Phelps would have said the conversation was interrupted by High, not a Def't, and who could be a witness; if false what need to say they were interrupted at all? how ridiculous to think he would name the person and furnish a witness to impeach himself. Nothing is more likely than that High would so interrupt a conversation at a public tavern and forget it. What was to fix it in his memory? A mere passing remark. Not so with Phelps; he was keeping a regular diary—the details of every occurrence he has given, show how full and accurate a one; every trivial thing was fixed in his memory. It is almost as absurd to suppose that High could remember a common place remark made over six months ago, as to suppose that a man like Phelps would voluntarily furnish a witness, who if he were false would unquestionably prove him so.

5. At page 128 Phelps narrates the substance of an interview between himself and Fitch at the Centre as follows:

[Here counsel read the testimony.]

It is claimed that Wm. B. Laycock disproves the possibility of this conversation having taken place.

Here is the testimony of Laycock,

[Here the counsel read the testimony.]

You perceive gentlemen, that the two witnesses agree in many essential particulars. They argree as to an interview, and the time and place of its occurrence. They agree as to the persons present, Phelps, Fitch, Filley, Ackerson and Laycock. Both agree that there was a good deal of conversation between Phelps and Fitch about buying and selling the oxen; the only pretence of a contradiction is that Phelps says they spoke of the Niles affair and the burning at Detroit, and Laycock says he did not hear this and that he heard all the conversation. There is no pretence that W. B. Laycock ever belonged to the combination, therefore if such conversation did occur he would not be permitted to hear it. That is certain. According to Phelps, he and Fitch had agreed on $200 for burning the depot; the only thing remaining to be settled between them was how much should be allowed for the cattle. Fitch asking $160, Phelps first insisting on $100 and afterwards offering to allow $120. At page 143 Phelps says, they spoke about the cattle in the ball alley "and afterwards had some loud or public talk about the price of the cattle but not in connection with the Niles affair." Is not this natural? Is it not the way in which the conversetion would be conducted? Of the Niles affair and the old burning; of every thing criminal they would speak privately, but, as to the mere price of the oxen there was nothing to prevent their speaking aloud. It is manifest then that if the conversation did occur as Phelps states Laycock's testimony would be just what it is. He would hear them chaffer about the price of the cattle, but would hear nothing of the criminal consideration. The only question is, can you rely on Laycock's testimony that he heard *every word* that passed? Laycock tells you "he was no way interested in the trade;" that they were 15 or 20 minutes in the ball alley; and 15 or 20 in the bar room after Fitch came: they moved from one place to another; the cars passed while they were there, and he went out to hold his horse; there was also some drinking; and yet without paying particular attention or anything to require him to do so, he tells you he heard every word that passed. He did not even join in the conversation. According to all ordinary experience the testimeny of Laycock, is more a corroboration than a contradiction, for it is just such testimony as he would give if Phelps is true; but over and beyond all this, why should Phelps invent this tale? it is quite unnecessary; it implicates no one but Fitch, and Fitch is fully identified and implicated in half a dozen other interviews both by Phelps and Lake. Again Loycock says, "he heard every work spoken and has repeated all," yet all he repeats does not occupy over a minute in the delivery, and Phelps and Fitch were there over half an hour. Laycock may after six months imagine he heard all, and probably did hear all that was not spoken privately or in a low tone.

6. Ulysses T. Foster testifies that in the State Prison, in 1849, Phelps (pointing to Fitch, who was passing by) said: "He is the means of my being here; I will have revenge or satisfaction." Calvin Beebe says that in April, 1849, when he announced to Phelps that a pardon had been granted to him, he replied: "I am in prison through the influence of Abel F. Fitch and others. If I live to get out, I'll make them smart for it, and give them the same feed they have given me."

Phelps said he did not recollect using this language; and we must meet it as we best can. I have not yet, and I will not now, seek to shake any testimony by charges, unless when I believe them well founded. I know of nothing against either Beebe or Foster. I see no reason why you should not credit their testimony. But it is remarkable, and I beg of you to note it gentlemen, that altho.' by the course of examination you were given to understand that Phelps would be contradicted in *material matters*, relative to which he could not be mistaken or forgetful, the contradicting witnesses were never called, or when called the transparent falsity of their testimony, worked evil not good for the defence. To these matters I will have to call your attention at the proper time; at present I have to deal with the testimony of Foster and Beebe; and show you that much as it has been harped upon it amounts to but little or nothing. It is material only as indicating malice or want of truthfulness in Phelps. If the words were the ebulition of sudden feeling, passing away leaving no festering malice behind, and *forgotten* when they passed from the lips that uttered them, they are utterly immaterial—divested of malice they are immaterial of thtmselves—*forgotten* there is no want of truthfulness in denying their use. Was there malice? Gentlemen, embittered words do not always spring from a heart boiling with malice or revenge—they are often the offspring of indignation or erroneously conceived opinions. In the latter case cooler moments, or the correction of the error wipes out every trace of their existence; in the former the revengeful seed continues to send forth its natural fruit, and unceasingly betray its existence. How is it in this case? You know enough to be aware that Phelps believed that he was wrongfully imprisoned—that the executive concurred in that opinion and pardoned him, but for four years his tears had moistened the bread of a captive; for four years he had toiled within the gloomy walls of a prison, was it not natural—was it not human—that as he thought of his home his wife, his child, the sunlight that was denied him, and the pleasures beyond his reach, that his heart should frame and his lips utter bitter curses on the man whom he deemed had wrecked his every hope in life? But was Abel F. Fitch tnat man? No! for at page 143 Phelps says:

"Mr. Fitch was a witness for me when I was convicted and sent to State Prison, he was called to impeach a witness against me, and did it the most liberal manner; he took a decided interest in my behalf; I never had an ill feeling against Fitch, and never had any difficulty with him."

If this was not true, why was not Phelps contradicted? If Fitch was not a favorable witness why has it not been shown? If difficulty ever arose, why is it unproven? If Phelps entertained malice the only cause assigned is for aiding in his conviction—that is its nature, its reason, the one sole cause embodied in his threat. It often happens that the captive hears false accusations against his best friends. If they are breathed in his ear after four years of unmerited punishment, when the heart is crushed and the feelings morbid, they are readily received and believed in, and while they last excite bitter emotions. But if the accusation is false, 'tis soon corrected, and bitter feelings are forgotten. The whole course of Phelps' conduct after he left the Prison shows that such must have been the case between him and Fitch. He went to Prison in '44, then believing Fitch his friend, knowing that he was active to procure his acquittal. Every friend that visited him had some suspicion to breathe against one person or another; and during these four years he had probably accused a hundred persons as the instruments of his incarceration. It finally became Fitch's turn to be suspected—he *was* suspected. And while suspicion existed the threat was breathed "he is the means of my being here." "I am here through his influence, and will give him the same feed." Perhaps the words of the next friend that visited him, or the next moments reflection on Fitch's favorable services at the trial, erased the suspicion, and blotted out the hasty anger it engendered. This is no improbable hypothesis, and it alone is reconcilable with the facts and after conduct of Phelps. He suspected Fitch wrongfully, that is conceded, for was it otherwise, there could be no excuse for counsel failing to prove it. Phelps' conduct shows that he corrected this erroneous suspicion. For two years after coming from prison he lived within 8 or 10 miles of Fitch. Does he attempt to do him any injury? No. Does he during these two years breathe a threat, or lisp a syllable against Fitch? Not one. It is only after a lapse of two years that we find him near Fitch, and then at his own house, by his *own* request.—Can it be believed that malice festered in his heart during these two years, and yet while hundreds of his neighbors, and daily associates, have been on the stand, there is not one who ever saw or detected the slightest indication of it. 'Tis an absurdity if not an impossibility.—Again, if the the threat sprung from hastily assumed and as hastily abandoned suspicion, Phelps might easily have forgotten it, but if from deep enduring malice that could burn and glow and live through two years, without food or outward indication, he could not have forgotten and would know that two truthful witnesses would contradict him. In such a case how easily this man (described by counsel as possessing the cunning of a devil) could have broken the force of the contradiction by "I once suspected him, and may have said something of the kind," or one of a hundred other such sentences.

7. At page 122 Phelps gives an account of an interview with Fitch at his barn in the month of December, as follows.

(Here counsel read the testimony.)

On cross-examination he states that on this occasion he went to the Centre with some of the Lacocks, and after it returned to Lacock's.

It is claimed that his account of this interview is contradicted by Morgan S. Lacock, H. T. Lacock and C. Blackburn, whose testimony I read.

(Here counsel read portions of the testimony.)

You perceive that about the fact of an interview there is no difference. They all agree that on that day Phelps went to the Centre, and that after he arrived at Filley's he went alone to Fitch's for the purpose, as he said, of seeing him about the oxen. So far the witnesses all corroborate each other, but Pnelps said he was *two hours* at Fitch's and it is claimed the other testimony limits the time he was at Fitch's to half an hour. Now all that Phelps has narrated might pass in less than half an hour, and it is scarce a contradiction to find a witness mistaken when he gives an opinion as to the duration of an interview. Even the witnesses who are claimed to contradict *him*, in this respect contradict each other, for they each assign a different hour as the time when they returned. Your own experience will tell you how seldom, even, persons present at the same interview will agree in a statement of its length. The counsel is mistaken in saying that Phelps said the interview was in the afternoon. I have looked carefully over his testimony and find no such such statement. If Phelps had noted his interview with a time piece, and the others had done the same, and then differed materially there might, be an excuse to claim a contradiction, but none of the parties appear to have had watches. There is no reason assigned why any should note the lapse of lime; they *all* give their *impressions* six months after the occurrence, upon a matter which of all others would be likely to involve an honest dlfference of opinion, and which is utterly immaterial.

8. Of a similar character is the pretended conversation between Phelps and his wife at the house of W. B. Laycock. Laycock says that after they went to bed Phelps and his wife whispered over an hour and Phelps said aloud "if Wescott does as he agreed I will come a good drive on Fitch;" he tells you that altho' they whispered over an hour, this was all that was spoken aloud; he tells you they all slept in the same room, their beds almost touching each other and that Phelps was aware he was there. The absurdity of this story is an answer to it, for it is utterly absurd, to suppose that a man entertaining the designs imputed to Phelps would thus reveal them. But to set the matter at rest we placed Mrs. Phelps on the stand, and she, as you heard, denied that there was any such conversation. Laycock also says that on his return from the Centre Phelps said he "would have Fitch in the limbo for not selling him the cattle," and this is no less an absurdity than the other. The counsel stated that even the wife of the man, Phelps, would not swear certainly that the conversation did not occur, but only she *thought* not. Gentlemen all you have to do is to turn to your books, read her whole testimony and detect this misrepresentation.

9. The learned counsel says Phelps contradicts himself by saying that when he saw the match in January at the Centre he told Fitch and Filley he had seen a similar one at Gay's; when in another portion of his testimony he says he did not see the one at Gay's till February. I refer you to the entire passage in Phelps testimony, page 148 and you see he is guilty of no such blunder.

"When the machine was shown me at the Centre, I told them I had seen one like it at Gay's; saw it at Gay's house on the night of the 24th of February, in a small bedroom, on the left hand, up the first flight of stairs."

The entire sentence shows that he referred to a period subsequent to the 24th February, probably to the time when he got the Niles match.

And these were the fatal engines which were to destroy Phelps!

I have now gentlemen, gone thro' with all the alleged contradictions of Phelps' so far as my minutes of the counsel's argument can suggest them, with the exception of those pertaining to the eleventh of April, and which will be more conveniently treated of, as I proceed with a review of his testimony. By grouping all of these pretended contradictions together, I have placed them before your minds in the strongest light, and I ask you what do they all amount to? There is not one among them of much materiality, even if the contradiction was established, and such as they are the other evidence explains them away. You remember the general outline of Phelps testimony; you remember its length; the variety of its details; the number of its incidents; the almost numberless places and interviews it comprized; you will perceive at once that if false he exposed himself to material and substantial, and essential contradictions at every step, yet no such contradictions have been shown. When a witness deposes to such a quantity and variety of matter involving so many occurrences and individuals it would be strange indeed if some were not found whose recollections would differ from his as to the hour, the date, or some such immaterial matters,and these are the only points on which a contradiction is attempted. To find the substantial portion of a witness's testimony remains uncontradicted is always an evidence of truth which cannot be overborne by a difference of opinion between witnesses in matters immaterial to the issue.

Having thus, gentlemen, I trust to your entire satisfaction, shown that Phelps stands before you unimpeached by general character or contradictions, I will, for a moment, call your attention to those matters wherein he stands uncontradicted, notwithstanding that, either in the opening for the defence, or by questions put to him in the usual form for impeachment, the defence intimated their ability to contradict him.

These matters will also serve to illustrate the difference between material and immaterial matters.

You were promised, in the opening, that proof would be adduced that Phelps and Lake while in prison, entered into an agreement that when they got out, they would make fortunes by burning buildings and swearing the crimes on to innocent parties. No such proof has been offered. At page 145, Phelps was asked if they had not entered into that agreement; he denied it, and no attempt has been made to contradict it. When recalled for cross-examination he was asked if he had not, in September, tried to hire John Hawley to aid in burning the Detroit depot, and swearing it on to those who had cattle killed, promising him $50 and a portion of the reward—he denied it. Hawley was sworn, and testified he had so tried to hire him; but in a few days after, stung by the restless gnawings of remorse, he begged to be recalled upon the stand. He was again placed before you, pale and trembling, and confessed that his evidence was deliberate perjury, to which he was suborned by Billings, the friend and partizan of these defendants. The same Mr. Billings who, by turning to page 98, you will find was to have impeached another of our witnesses, if the fate of his pupil Hawley had not warned him that the moment he appeared in this county, he would be placed in the custody of the law until he had expiated his crimes.

At page 159, Phelps was asked if he had not tried to hire George Lynx and Andrew Barney, for $200, to swear that Lemn had fired the depot. He denied it; yet no Lynx or Barney appeared to contradict him.

At the same page; he was asked if he had not tried to hire Bildad Bennett to swear against Fitch, Burnett, et. al. He denied it; yet although all through the trial actively engaged for the defence, no Bildad Bennett appeared to contradict him.

At page 150, Phelps was asked if he had tried to hire Smith, by letter and personal application, to go out and get acqnainted with the defendants in order to swear against them, or to swear Lemn burned the depot. He denied it; yet there was no attempt to contradict him.

On July 15th, when recalled for cross-examination, he was asked if he had not tried to hire Cooper to rob the depot safe. He denied it, but charged that Cooper tried to seduce him into the commission of crime, that he might be arrested, and that even one or more of the counsel for defendants were cognizant of the plot. Mr. Cooper was not produced to contradict him by the defence, but at much cost and trouble the prosecution brought Cooper from his hiding place, placed him on the stand, and the defence availed itself of technical grounds to exclude his evidence.

On July 14th, he was asked if he had not said to one Dyer, that he was bound to break up Fitch and his band, even by false swearing, and to have revenge. He denied it. Dyer was placed upon the stand, and it was claimed, contradicted him. But when Hawley was arrested Dyer disappeared; he did not even wait for cross-examination, although his evidence was important enough to justify the trouble and expense of bringing him from Indiana; it was deemed more prudent to assent that it should be stricken out, than that he should be produced for cross-examination, and arrested for wilful perjury.

On the same day he was asked if he had not solicited Miss Merwin to go to Fitch's and leave counterfeit money on his premises. He denied it. Explained that his only purpose in going to Merwin's was to ascertain for the sheriff if she was not living in a state of incest with her father; and yet, although as appears by the confession of Hawley, Miss Merwin was in town, brought here from Indiana to impeach him; she is never produced.

I might with little trouble add to the list of important contraditions that were shadowed forth and promised, but I have given you enough to exhibit the marked contrast that exists between those attempted and those left unattempted. You will perceive that if the witnesses named in the list of questions I have read were produced, and contradicted Phelps, their testimony, if believed, would have gone far to establish the whole theory of the defence. It would have shown Phelps and Lake conspired to burn buildings, and swear their arsons on to others. It would have shown Phelps, in September, plotting the burning of the depot, with the design of charging it upon these defendants. It would have shown him on divers occasions, suborning witnesses to swear falsely against them. It would have shown him expressing bitter malice and hatred against these defendants, and Fitch in particular. In a word, gentlemen, it would have come up in letter and in spirit to the evidence promised by counsel in their opening. But it is all abandoned, and in its stead you are offered a few alleged contradictions upon matters without the case, totally immaterial in themselves—of a character where honest witnesses are frequently mistaken; and even these arising from a mistaken view of the testimony, or answered fully by their own inherent improbability.

And now, gentlemen, that we find Phelps unimpeached, and uncontradicted, without falsehood on his tongue, or malice in his heart, how is it with his testimony? If we find that it is sustained page by page, and line by line, by other witnesses, with whom he could by no possibility have collusion; if we find it natural in itself, devoid of all improbabilities, and dotted over with the inherent evidences of truth, I will feel every assurance in asking you to receive it as true. It may prove wearisome to an audience, that I should go over, even hurriedly, the testimony of Phelps; but I am convinced it will not prove so to you; anxious as I know you are to do your duty, fairly and faithfully, and render a verdict that your consciences will approve, you wiil cheerfully endure every dull detail, that may the better enable you to come to a just conclusion. As we pass over the important portions of his testimony, you will perceive that it is fully corroborated, and that if false, a hundred doors are opened for contradictions upon material points. You will, I have no doubt, come to the same conclusion I have arrived at, that from the very nature of his testimony, it is quite impossible that he should be at the same time untrue and uncontradicted.

He testifies that in December he had an interview with Fitch at the Centre, in which Fitch proposed to him to burn one or the other of four depots; that he wanted it done by some shrewd man, &c. Wescott proves that the same proposition had been made to him, by Fitch; and Loud proves that Corwin, who with Fitch, I have shown you was clearly identified in the combination, intimated that there would soon be a fire at the Jackson depot. McMichael and Morgan Wescott also prove the intention to burn the Jackson depot; and Dobbs proves the proposition on the part of several of the defendants to burn the boats of the Company. We have the same designs and intentions on the part of the conspirators, of which Fitch was undoubtedly the leader. And why should we doubt that the proposition was made to Phelps as he states. The fact of this interview having taken place, is proven by their own witnesses, though they differ as to the time of its duration.

Again, he says, Fitch urged upon him that he was already ruined in the eyes of community, and that if he went into their plans they would place him in easier circumstances. Are not these the very reasons that would present themselves to such a man as Fitch, to tempt one who had once borne the badge of ruin and disgrace? You are told it was not likely that a country gentleman like Fitch, "would thus commit himself to a pardoned convict; but you will remember there are a host of unassailed witnesses who prove that the heart of this country gentleman was filled with malevolence against this road; nor will you forget the actual intimacy between Fitch and Phelps so fully proven.— It is certain that if Fitch did not actually participate in, he knew of and encouraged the perpetration of injuries against it, far more fearful in their consequences, than the burning of the Depot. The country gentlemen whose rural sport it was to obstruct trains, and according to his own confession, to arm savage boys with pistols to "frighten engineers and passengers," needed other hands than his own to work out his designs; and I ask you was not Phelps just the man he would select. He was shrewd, sober and intelligent; he might readily be supposed to have a morbid hatred of the world, but above all he *had* been a convict; the brand of crime had once been stamped upon him, and if he dared betray, he could be crushed. In the words which a dozen witnesses have given you as the language of these conspirators he could "be sworn down." Again you will note that in this interview, no confession was made of the past arson; it was only afterwards, when Phelps seemed caught by the tempting bait, and firmly hooked, that he was admitted to full confidence.

Again he says, Fitch said the road was a curse to the community and he and others had determined to see the people's wrongs righted; the Company had already been injured, and they desired to go farther to bring them to terms. If not from Fitch himself, where did Phelps learn this language; this straining to throw the garb of heroism and public spirit, over fiendish crimes; thus ascribing lofty motives to the burning of Depots, and the murdering of women *and children.* That they were Fitch's sentiments, there is no doubt, for so precisely, he expresses himself Attorney-General Lothrop, to Wm. Gibson, to Wm. Galespie and others; witnesses from whom Phelps could not have learned them for he had no communion with them. The most important interview to which he testifies is on Christmas day at Filleys; he says Filley said he thought Fitch would give the oxen and the balance of $200 in cash if I would burn the Depot at Niles. You will note gentlemen, the consistency of this testimony, with that which has fallen froma hundred others. Brown told you they used to call Fitch Captain; when the proposal was made to Dobbs, Fitch was referred to as one who would pay; so McMichael says Fitch's name was used as an inducement to him to burn Jackson Depot: Wescott p. 43, says, Barrett said Fitch could always clear them; again Welling said Burnett told Fitch to stop the obstructions; but Fitch said he had advised the boys *not to get caught*—all indicating that Fitch was the man to pay the leader. And here again, with the harmony of truth itself, "Filley thought Fitch would give me the oxen and the balance in money."—And so, gentlemen, you will find it through all this testimony of Phelps; lengthy and minute as it is, there is not a word that clashes with the evidence of the 100 unassailed witnesses who have been sworn. He says at this interview, Filley told him they had sent a match to a man in Detroit, to put in the cupola, described the match, &c.

Here gentlemen, is the first confession of any connection with the fire in Detroit; by reading the full testimony, you will perceive that on on this day, E. Price also confessed to an aiding in the arson; and you will ask yourselves how strange it is, that while it is claimed that malice to Fitch was Phelp's great motive, he passes him by and identifies with the burning, two men against whom there is no pretence that he ever entertained a particle of enmity. You will also notice that while Corwin and others join in the conversation and urge him to undertake the Niles matter and other crimes against the road, he does not place words in the mouth of any one of them, save these two, that could implicate them with the arson. You will also perceive that at this early date he located the fire *in the cupola.* The importance of this is, that *although* when the persons who first saw the fire were hunted up and brought upon the stand, it was made manifest the fire was there; yet there were many who until then, would swear it was not. It was only the strict tests of oath and cross-examination, that established where the fire first was. You will bear in mind that Phelps is not shown to have been acquainted with the witnesses who have here proved that the fire did originate in the cupola; yet Phelps was told by defendants, that the match was there placed, and he reported the fact to the Company. There is also strong corroboration to the truth of Filley's confession of his participation in the arson—Mr. Sutton and Wm. Morrison, p. 108 and 9, say—Filley speaking of the burning of the Depot, said "I suppose they will lay it to me, God damn them; I will show the Company I *can burn out here as well as down there.*" So far as Ammi Filley is concerned, we might dispense with the testimony of Phelps altogether. Coming from a man engaged for years with outrages against the Company, and who had threatened to burn, and who as half a dozen men prove, gave the Company credit on the burning; this language to Suttonand Morrisonis a confession in itself. How natural it is that Filley who spoke so recklessly in a grocery in Jackson should be the first to entrust the secret to Phelps.

The next interview that Phelps testifies to, is, that at Palmers; where he states there was some conversation relative to Lacock's turning spy, and his having received pistols from Fitch to shoot at the cars. It is claimed that C. Blackburn swore this conversation never occurred.—Phelps named Blackburn as one of the persons present, and yet he does not from the beginning to the end, swear to a single word against him. Now if Phelps was swearing false, how easily he could have given some admissions to Blackburn that would at least seal his mouth as a witness. Yet although at one time Blackburn was a defendant, Phelps passes him over; does not attribute a single word to him, but leaves him to be discharged by the Court, and become a witness.—Again you will note how accurately he details all about the pistols given by Fitch, and how perfectly it corresponds with the truths that were then known only to a few, but which have since been revealed before you. You will bear in mind that this Blackburn was an idle, heedless boy; and that it may readily have been that he did not hear all that was said.

The next important testimony of Phelps is his interview at Leoni with Williams, Freeland, Corwin, and Price. Among other things,he says, plans were suggestod to get rid of Wells and Laycock who had gone into the employ of the Co., and Williams said, "you knew I was the means of the cars being thrown off altho' I was in bed." This you will note is early in January; but see how it corresponds with the testimony of other witnesses, some of them discovered since. Woliver says lt was done by Filley and the Prices; yet that Williams had a part in it is shown by Wescott who saw money paid to him on account of it. Williams afterwards explains to Lake that he remained in bed to be a witness and prove an alibi for those who did it; and Henry says when that obstruction was spoken of, Williams said "they couldn't lay it to him for he was in bed."

He further testifies that in this interview Freeland and Williams admitted the payment of money towards the burning in Detroit. Refer to the testimony and you can have little doubt that this is true.—Corwin told Loud "mark my words there will soon be a fire here," at the Jackson depot. He tried to induce McMichael to burn it, and he was one of those who tried to hire Dobbs to burn a steamboat; there is little doubt that the man who endeavored to have one depot burned would be party to the firing of another; and Brown and Wells and other witnesses have shown you that Freeland was a prominent man in the combination, and the first to whom the thought occurred of blowing up the train with powder.

The next important testimony is the interview with Fitch on the 10th of January. This is the interview claimed to be contradicted by W. B. Laycock, and referred to before among the alleged contradictions; and you will note that altho' it is said that animosity to Fitch and the desire to get him to prison was the chief object of Phelps, it is only at this late period after four others are implicated that any thing is revealed by Fitch to identify him with the arson. This is quite inconsistent with the theory of the defence: if malice against Fitch was his motive, and he spoke false, Fitch would be the first he would implicate ;and it is consistent with that which experience would lead us to expect,that the reckless tools would more freely commit themselves than the acute and cautious leader.

But to return to the interview between Phelps and Fitch. Phelps says he said they had prepared the match and sent it to a man in Detroit who placed it in the cupola; that they paid him $150.

This, gentlemen, was in January, yet how exactly it agrees with the admissions of Gay made in April, to Clark and Van Arman. Gay also says he got it from his friends at the Centre; he placed lt in the cupola, and they paid him $150.

To return to page 158 Fitch said it was "so constructed as to burn in a given time."

Is this not convincing evidence of truthfulness. We have shown you that match made according to the dascription given by Filley can be made"to burn a given time;" but were enabled to show it to you only by means of a skilful chemist. We have shown you in the most conclusive manner (I will not now repeat the argument on that point,) that Phelps was utterly ignorant of the material and construction of these matches; how then could he, so far back as January have put these words in the mouth of Fitch.

In this same interview Phelps says Fitch spoke of the injury already done to the company; of people having been warned not to travel; of his influence and his ability to procure witnesses; that he could impeach any man.

It is scarce necessary that I should ask you is not all this evidence true? The same in substance is testified to by a dozen witnesses who are not questioned; far more is testified to by Mr. Knickerbocker and Mr. Chadwick. The truth of much of it you have witnessed, yourselves so far back as January, Phelps reveals that that the chief bond and reliance among these men was their ability in case of of a prosecution to obtain false testimony. The arrest and prosecution came, and as promised, the perjury came with it. Hawley was subpoened. Although Dyer has not confessed, I am safe in saying he was not a true witness, else why should he, an important witness, fly the state without examination. I am also safe in saying that when the questions I have read to you were put to Phelps the witnesses were on hand to contradict him. They knew he would deny, and were prepared to contradict. Let me instance the case of Miss Merwin whom by Hawley's statement we know came here, and was in this city before the question relative to her was put to Phelps; before they knew he would deny it. She was sent for and brought to contradict him. What inference can you draw but this—that knowing he never said it, they knew he would deny it. Otherwise why not wait for his denial before bringing her from Indiana; but it is useless to argue that the defendants were prepared with false witnesses. We know that parson Billings brought his quota from Indiana, and before I conclude I will show you just as conclusively that Leoni furnished its quota, and fully justified the boast of Williams that they "had there those who could prove a horse a smith's shop, and every hair a lighted candle."

I will ask you here, gentlemen, to pause and review the portion of Phelps testimony which we have gone over. You percieve that up to this point he states many things that have since been otherwise demonstrated, and which in the month of January could have been known only to the initiated. As for instance. That the depot was fired in the cupola; that such a match as Filley described would and could be graduated to burn a given time; that Gay was the person who actually fired the depot; that if arrested and prosecuted, these defendants would defend themselves by false witnesses. Until the testimony in this case shed its light upon them, all these facts were involved in darkeess and doubt, how then could Phelps in January state them as facts. How account for his positive statements of these things in January save by the hypothesis that he speaks truly; that he had had his information from the men who made the match, and procured the commission of the arson?

You will remember that until after this period, Phelps was not in the employ of the Company, but in the employ of Mr. Bates—that up to this time he states he gave information to Mr. Bates of what he learned. Mr. Bates was in the court room frequently during this trial. If Phelps spoke falsely in saying he knew these things in January, the defendants had it in their power to contradict him, and failing to do so it is equally a rule of law and of common sense that you shall presume that if placed on the stand Mr. Bates would so far corroborate him.

It is proven that in January Phelps knew and stated with certainty many of the truths of this case of which all others were ignorant: a fact which can only be accounted for by the hypothesis that he is an honest witness and has spoken the truth. You will also remember that while the defence claim that the charge of arson was the pure result of malice against Fitch, Phelps testifies (and Mr. Bates could contradict him if it were untrue) that a few weeks after the depot was burned, he told Mr. Bates of Gay's confession that he was the felon; and only seeks further revelations by the direction of Mr. Bates. Yet although he is the first man against whom he gives information, counsel gravely tell you it was all a plot between Phelps and Gay.

But to return to the narrative of Phelps. He tells you that in February, Dr. Farnham told him that he was preparing a machine to blow up the track, and that in March he showed it to him, and said it was then complete. In going over the list of acts done, I have already shown you that this evidence is abundantly corroborated. By Brown and Wells, that the plan of using powder to blow up the track was contemplated by Freeland, Fitch, Filley and others, and by Wyman and Burdick that the Doctor was prepared to blow them up.

Phelps next details his interviews and conversations with Fitch in Detroit, and which, although attacked by the defence, are, as you have seen, fully established and corroboratad by Mr. Doane, Mr. Sheely and Wescott, and his long conversation with Fitch on his way home in the cars, which is also corroborated by Mr. White.

Before passing on I will allude to the substance of these conversations as detailed by Phelps.

1. Fitch came to make some arrangement to prevent Wells and Laycock making disclosures to the company. We afterwards find that Laycock *leaves* their employment. 2. Fitch says he gave Gay the matches to burn the depot. We afterwards find Gay telling Clark and VanArman that this is so, showing them a match and offering to take them to the Centre and introduce them to defendants, 3. He tells how he detected that Wescott was a spy. There could be no collusion here between Phelps and Wescott, as both deny acquaintance at the time, and if it existed the defence could prove it. And Phelps made regular and full reports to Mr. Clark, who had them in Court, within the control of the defence; and yet his account is substantially the same as Wescott's, the only variance being, that while Wescott and several other witnesses show the information of his being a spy, to have been given by the prison guard, Fitch boasts to Phelps that it was sent by the Prison agent himself, Fitch you will perceive where he gave the narration, was boasting of his influence, and it was very natural that he should substitute the *agent* for the *guard*. It is a variance, but a variance that rather confirms than weakens the truth of the evidence.

The next important evidence is the interview of Phelps with several of the defendants, at Bascom's tavern on the first day of the Court. He says they had a long private conversation in the sitting-room, and this fact is corroborated by George Holden, a constable, who went in to serve a subpœna. Apart from the corroboration, the mind naturally inquires if there were no criminal secrets between these men and Phelps, why all these secret interviews corroborated by so many witnesses? Why should Fitch subsequently say he knew Phelps but slightly? It was at this time that Lake was introduced as the person to assist at the Niles' burning, and when Williams stated the rules to be that if he betrayed he should be shot. Although Williams proposed swearing Lake to secrecy, Lake only pledged himself. This is seized upon by the counsel as evidence of the falsity of the whole scene; he asks why was not the oath insisted on if it was the rule? Who deputed Williams to represent the entire combination, receive the neophyte and administer the oath?

To my mind it is evidence of directly the reverse, for if Phelps was fabricating, he would have colored the scene; there would be more secresy, more form and probably an oath; but as he tells it, it is entirely consistent with the testimony of others. These men had no lodge, no officers, no forms of initiation, but whenever a new conspirator joined them, he was was warned that punishment and vengeance would follow a betrayal. But again, Phelps says that in this interview Williams said they were going to make a proposition through their attorney to the company for a settlement, We offered to prove that such a proposition was made, but it was objected to—the offer over-ruled. We named and placed upon the stand the witness to whom it was made, and the defendants had it amply in their power to show the falsity of the witness. They could show if no such proposition was made, or by calling for Phelps' reports to Clark, could show if he had not reported their intention before their offer was made. How is this to be answered, save by the hypothesis that Phelps speaks the truth? Did he prophecy such a proposal, and then influence the defendants—innocent men, who never violated a law—to work its fulfilment by implicating themselves?

Again, he testifies to his interview with Gunn at Niles, and if you turn to the testimony of Mr. Fitzmorris, you will find it fully corroborated, not merely as to the interview, but as to a portion of the conversation about getting Sherman out of the way, Again, on page 137 he says, that as early as March the boys informed him that they were all working for particular candidates for the approaching election, and strange enough those very candidates got almost the unanimous vote of Leoni, although of opposite politics to the usual vote of the town. We find Phelps prophesying against all seeming probabilities, but his prophecies are always fulfilled.

I have thus, gentlemen, taken the most important portions of his testimony and shown you that it is wondrously corroborated. I might go over it all in the same manner. There is scarcely a line that is not sustained by other witnesses, but I dare not trespass longer on your time, and pass on to his testimony regarding the 11th of April.

Without delaying you by reading his testimony in full you will remember that in substance he and Lake testify that on the morning of the 11th of April, they left Metcalf's in a buggy; that they had nothing in the buggy but some straw; that they went to the house of G. Cady to see about a horse Phelps wished to purchase; and from thence along the road that runs north of Beeman's field, and about a mile south of Leoni, (not going through Leoni,) to the Centre. That they did not part, or get out of the buggy from leaving Cady's till they reached the Centre; they then saw Filley; Lake being sick, remained there; and Phelps at once went to Leoni; thence to Grass Lake; back to Leoni, and from thence in the evening, accompanied by Myers and Corwin to the Centre, where the match for the burning of the Niles depot was delivered.

The principal portion of the defendants testimony has been intended to contradict Phelp's in his narration of his journey and the occurrences of this day. The effort of all the testimony has been to raise a presumption that Phelps and Lake carried the match to the Centre on this 11th of April, making as the counsel claims, a third distinct defence. From all the indications we had, we could easily anticipate, that Leoni would "do its duty" towards these defendants, and her champions selected the space between Cady's and the Centre for a battle-ground. It now becomes my duty to carefully examine the evidence adduced by the defendants upon this head, and show that while a portion of it is the result of evident mistake; the balance is wilful and deliberate falsehood; just of the character that could prove "every hair in a horse a lighted candle."

I. It is claimed that they carried a box tied up in a red kerchief in the buggy; that Cady, Peeler and Kellogg saw it.

7*

I now refer to the testimony of Mr. Cady. (Here counsel read portions of Cady's testimony.)

You see gentlemen that Mr. Cady, who is evidently an honest upright man, does not color his testimony. He tells you he cannot be certain he saw anything in the buggy; but is of the impression that there was a "reddish *bundle*" back of the seat. You will remember that when recalled Lake testified that he had with him that day, an overcoat with red lining which he produced, and the day being warm it was thrown off. But counsel says this was an afterthought; but by turning to the cross-examination of Mr. Cady you will perceive one of the first questions asked him was if it was not an overcoat he saw, and he replied "It *might* be an overcoat." There is so far no contradiction; it was not strange that Phelps and Lake should at first omit to state they had an overcoat, any more than that they should omit to state they had undercoats, or boots, or any other article of dress. You have heard that Mr. Cady stood several minutes beside them in the road. If they had a square box in a red handkerchief, it would give a very different idea from a "*bundle like*," and one that would never permit him to say "it might be an overcoat." I now turn to the testimony of Peeler and Kellogg.

(Here counsel read the testimony.)

You perceive they had no such opportunity to see what was in the buggy as Mr. Cady; they merely passed Phelps and Lake on the highway without stopping, while Cady drew up beside them in the road and conversed for several minutes. Yet Peeler and Kellogg swear, one that it was "the shape of a box;" the other, "something in a square form." They tell you it excited their attention and they conversed about it. Suppose it to have been a box tied in a red hankerchief; is it at all probable that it would excite attention? Is it so unusual for two travelers in a buggy to have a small box in the back part of it? But listen to Peeler, "Kellogg said by G—d, he believed it was full of counterfeit money." Mr. Kellogg don't seem to quite relish the idea of fathering such profanity and gives a more subdued and chaste version he says, "I said perhaps the stranger is a *musician* and it belongs to him, perhaps it is a box of bogus or the tools for making it." This evidence you will remember was given before the arrest of Hawley. Before the prosecution had been guilty of the shameful oppression of arresting a miserable perjurer, and thus sending a bevy of witnesses back *unsworn* to the tamaracks of Indiana. It was the first gentle opening to all that *was to have been proved.* You will remember the counsel who opened promised to prove Phelps represented to Corwin the box contained bogus; it was therefore well enough to have other witnesses who not only saw the box but recognized in it the "bogus look," that helped to deceive Corwin. Where plain direct perjury has been shown on the part of the defence, as has been done in this case, you are bound to look with caution if not suspicion on all their testimony. Perjury was one of the weapons of defence. Is not this a likely place to strike a blow with it? The witnesses only swear they deemed it a box, and who could indict them for mistaking a bundle for a box? They would be safe in stretching their testimony a little. But are they men who would do it? Listen to Peeler's biography of himself. He entered the army, was twice Court Matialled, and finally punished and dismissed from the service. He contracted an alliance by soldiers marriage with a woman at Sackets Harbor; they had a child; he left them and never inquired after them since, and don't know if they are living or dead. He married again at the Sault; can't tell his wifes name or if she had another husband living when he married her, but heard something of the kind; can't tell who married him or who were present; he came to Detroit, lived with Kellogg and finally the pair found a suitable home and settled down like brothers in the same house and near the rural district of Leoni. You can review their testimony gentlemen and determine whether they have spoken falsely, or only stretched a little for friendship's sake or whether they are honestly mistaken, taking into account the improbability that Phelps and Lake would thus carry a match exposed to the view of every passer by.

The next alleged contradiction is while Phelps says he did not go to the village of Leoni till after he left Lake at the Centre about noon, several witnesses swore they saw him in Leoni on that day from 10 to 12 o'clock; that he came in from the South, and his horse ran away.— These witnesses are Alden Luce, Mrs. Tull, Jno. Cuykendall, and I. D. Tull. All of these witnesses save Mrs. Tull, identify the occasion as the day of a certain lawsuit before Justice Bildad Bennett, a gentleman whose name has already figured in this cause as one of the witnesses who *did'nt* swear; and who will again appear as active in procuring the testimony of the Bemans, which I will show you to a moral certainty is false. You will remember that Phelps on being recalled testified that on an occasion preceding the 11th, he did come into Leoni from the South, and his horse did run as described. The question then becomes one of date, and while three of the four witnesses swear that they were guided by the date of the suit, as it was in the possession of a warm friend, it would have been frank and candid to have produced the docket, and shown that there was no mistake in the date; that there were no erasures, no attempt to mislead by a skilful change of the date of the suit' It can scarce be expected that a prosecution can demonstrate that every particle of testimony introduced by a defence, springs from mistake or want of truth, but in this instance it can be done.

I refer you to the testimony of Mr. Luce who swears he saw Phelps as described on the 11th. "He knows it was the eleventh because it was the day of the suit. And he has since examined the record."— So far it is consistent enough, but follow his cross examination and he tells you that about sunrise on the Thursday following the eleventh, he met Phelps on the railroad track near Leoni. "He *knows* this was the Thursday after the 11th;" and gives you divers reasons why he cannot be mistaken. Turn to the testimony of Mr. Howe and Mr. Spaulding given the 1st of Sept., and you find beyond all dispute that Phelps was in Detroit Wednesday night and Thursday morning, and that he went West on a train that followed the regular one on Thursday morning. So he could not by any possibility be where Luce says he met him before noon on that day. Luce then is mistaken beyond question, and it follows that the other two who swear by the docket are also mistaken. Other circumstances show that Mrs. Tull, who does not swear by the docket, is also mistaken in the date. Her testimony in effect is that she saw Phelps come into Leoni a little past ten; after this she herself went to the Centre, and got there about 12 o'clock, when she arrived there she saw "the same horse and buggy Phelps had tied to the post, and in about three quarters of an hour after *the horse and buggy driven off South.*" There is something strange in this guarded phraseology; if she saw the horse and buggy driven off she saw who drove, and why not say it was Phelps or it was not Phelps. Although she may have been at the Centre on that day, and met Phelps, Corwin and Myers, on her return in the evening, as she states, it is very clear that it was not this day she saw Phelps in Leoni,and "the same horse and buggy" at the Centre for three quarters of an hour. Turn to the testimony of Mr. Kane, and Mr. Allen, both called by the defendants, young merchants of intelligence, and they tell you, they arrived at Filley's on the 11th, about noon or a very little past noon, and remained there till about 1 P. M., when they went to hunt. And although this is just the period when Mrs. Tull tells you the horse and buggy were there, they saw no such thing. And although they were round there making their preparations during the same period, Mrs. Tull never saw them; their vision was closed to the horse and buggy, while Mrs. Tull could see nothing else. It is manifest that she is mistaken, and the most charitable conclusion you can draw is that in her mind the occurrences of seveaal different days are by some strange confusion gathered into one—thus alone can you reconcile her testimony with that of others and preserve her character for truth. The learned counsel has referred to the testimony of Hudson, and says he proved that Phelps said at the Centre that night that his horse had run THAT day and it was the only time he ever did run. The counsel is mistaken in this; all Hudson says is "Phelps also said that his horse had run away, but that before he had been very steady." And this might as well apply to any other day as the 11th April.

We now come to the most important contradiction of all—an event in this case which fully illustrates the difficulty of framing a lie so simple that it does not bear the impress of falsity.

Lake and Phelps testify that they did not part till they got to the Centre—that Lake did not get out opposite the Beeman field, take a bundle out of the buggy, and go across lots towards the Centre. On the other hand, James E. Secord, David Beeman and Charles E. H. Beeman swear that at that point, on that day, and between 10 and 11 o'clock, they saw two persons answering to the description of Phelps and Lake, come along in a buggy, that the buggy stopped and one got out, took from it a bundle covered with a red handkerchief, and passed over the fence and through the fields towards the Centre, while the other person remained in the buggy and drove on to Leoni; and Taylor swears that on the same day, he met a man on the road between there and the Centre with a bundle covered with a red handkerchief under his arm.

The first thing that will strike you in reference to this testimony, is that it is confined to a single point. If the witnesses are false there would seem scarcely any possibility of contradicting them, there are no surrounding circumstances, no details, it does not, like the testimony of Phelps, embrace several persons and long details; it is confined merely to seeing a man get out of a buggy at a particular time and place. If then, in a tale so simple and so concise. we find that the witnesses get confused, contradict themselves and each other, and that the story bears every impress of improbability, painful though it may be, we cannot avoid the conviction that it is false. With these remarks I call your attention first to the testimony of Secord. By referring to his testimony you will perceive that he contradicts himself as follows: He says he told Cozzens of it, (seeing the man get out of the buggy) before Phelps was sworn, and again he says he can't say he ever spoke of it until *after* Phelps was sworn. Again, that for three or four weeks he has calculated to swear to this fact, and again, that until the day before he was on the stand, he did not keow it would be important. Again, he says he first thought his testimony would be important as he saw Phelps go from Leoni that night with Myers, and pay a quarter for liquor, and then he says he don't know why he thought *that* would be important. Here I will ask you to notice, gentlemen, that no mention was made about Phelps paying for liquor till on the 12th of July, by Luce, some nine days before Secord testified, and yet for four weeks he thought it would be important! Again, on his direct examination, he says he saw the man thus get out of the buggy from the 7th to the 11th, but on cross-examination fixes it on the 11th, and then don't remember if he said from the 7th to the 11th, and yet he fixes the date by the law suit before Bildad Bennett. These contradictions are all scattered through his cross-examination; they are not all in one place, but they are all *there*.

I next refer you to the testimony of David Beeman, who you will find contradicts himself as follows. He tells you he was at work with his son, and sent the lad to see if there were cattle in the field, and followed to see what delayed him, but when he saw the buggy, stopped to look after it, and although he did not think there was anything uncommon about what he saw, went back without looking farther after, or seeing, his son. He says Phelps passed first and Cozier passed 10 or 15 minutes after him, and again he says Cozier passed *before* Phelps. Again, he says he did not see Cozier till he got to the corners, and again, he first saw Cozier's wagon fifteen or twenty rods before it got to the corners. Again he tells you Phelps passed before Cozier, and Cozier overtook and passed him, yet Cozier, he says, went *slower* than Phelps. Again he tells you he saw Secord on Saturday, but he didn't tell and he don't know what he swore to. Again, he says Higby told him what *Secord swore to*, and yet again, he says Secord told him all about it, the place, the color of the horse, the dress of the man who got out, &c. Then again he tells you the only reason he noticed the man get out, was "because the road would be shorter to go to Michigan Centre, than to go across the lot." This was an incautious expression, it shows the witness assigning as a reason what could not strike his mind; this place is four miles from the Centre, houses and mills are scattered all along the way, and how could he conclude the man was going to the Centre, or think he had better have taken the road. I might add to the contradictions of this witness, but I have given enough to show you that he came to swear to a solitary point, and the moment he was led from that, he was at sea and swore at random.

I must refer you to the testimony of C. H. E.Beeman. In this witness we find few palpable contradictions of himself; he is an intelligent, cunning lad, and doubtless profited by the experience of others; indeed he tells us as much. You will remember the pert, self-satisfied air with which he exclaimed, he had asked his father on leaving the stand, "if they had laid him out, and told him if they hurt me, I will cut my head off." He came armed for the encounter; and it will certainly strike you that a lad of his age coming to swear to the truth, and that truth one single simple fact, would not thus prepare himself to "cut his head off if laid out." He also tells you, that until inquired of a few days before he came on the stand, by Bildad Bennett, "he never told what he saw. He had made up his mind not to tell unless he was asked." Is it not passing strange, that a boy seeing a man get out of a buggy would make up his mind never to tell of it? There is something so peculiar in the manner in which he tells of his having first revealed this secret that I willl readit to you. He says on the Wednesday before he was examined, "My father and I were loading wheat, and he he had started home when Bennett and Cozier came and called me to the fence. Bennett asked me if I knew anything of two men coming along, and one getting out and over the fence, and I told him just as I have told here. He said he knew I was at work fencing there at the time, and I must have seen the men come along. Before he asked me any questions, *he told me he knew I was at work*, and must have seen Phelps and the other man come along in a buggy, and then asked if I didn't see them." He can scarce be censured for so easily breaking his vows of secrecy to one who like Bennett could *tell him all he saw.* Again he tells you he did'nt want to be a witness; but yet he expected they would come for him, altho' he never told what he saw. There are fewer palpable self-contradictions on the part of this witness than the others, but if you glance over his testimony, you will perceive that there is a wavering air of insincerity pervading it that goes far to stamp the entire as false.

I next refer you to the testimony of E. Taylor, who you will find contradicts himself as follows. He says after Beeman had testified he had a conversation with him; he told Beeman he saw the *same* man, and again says he did not say the *same* man. He tells you he did not tell Beeman the man had a bundle with a red handkerchief; pressed a little farther on cross examination he says he told Beeman the man had a bundle; that there was a red handkerchief on it,and that the man was rather tallish. He tells you that on this day Penfield was at Detroit under arrest and seeing the blunder, he says he is mistaken in that, but he was away somewhere. He says he met Ladue near the mill and spoke to him about paying a debt in lumber, but he don't remember what answer Ladue gave; again he says Ladue said he sawed some at the mill; and again he don't know if Ladue ever attended the mill.

I do not wish you to suppose, gentlemen that in these I have given all the self contradictions of these witnesses. I have noted others but I dare not tresspass too far upon your time and hurry on to point out some things in which they could not well be mistaken or forgetful and in which they contradict each other. Old Beeman says, when he saw the buggey he looked no farther after his son but he returned to him in the field after a little. Young Beeman says his father followed him to the house and brought him back to the field. Old Beeman saw no wagon but Cozier; young Beeman says Zeikels had a second wagon and was between Cozier and Phelps. Young Beeman says that it was only after he heard the testimony of Phelps, he made up his mind not to tell what he saw. Taylor says the week of the arrest he asked young Beeman if he had seen a man with a bundle along there, and B. said he had not. Old Beeman says he never spoke a word of what he saw to any one till he told it to Higby on Saturday. Young Beeman says he and his father spoke of it on Wednesday after he saw Bennett; that they went together on Thursday and fixed on the spot where the man got out;and they went there again afterwards; yet they don't appear to remember the spot agreed on, for young Beeman says they got out before they passed the pond; old Beeman says after they passed it.

These contradictions may seem trivial in themselves, but you must remember, gentlemen, that where witnesses swear to a short and simple story, easily agreed on, their falsity must remain undiscovered, or be revealed by trivial surrounding matters. We could not hope to shake them, as to the man having got out of the buggy; that we knew they had agreed on; but in every trifling detail, that would not probably be agreed on beforehand, we find they wander and contradict themselves or each other. In reference to the two Beemans, I will remark that they are distinctly contradictedby other witnesses—Mr. Chapman, Mr. Spaulding and a number of others who went to the field, and testify, that from where the old man says he was at work, he had a full view, and could see his son all. the way to the place where the son stood, while he says he quit work in search of him. These witnesses placed themselves on the identical spots where old and young Beeman say they stood, and saw the man get out of the buggy, and tell you if they had been there as they state, they must have seen each other—yet one says he was looking for the other. They also tell you that old Beeman could not have seen Cozier's wagon in the place he states; and that young Beeman could not have seen it pass by Phelps, as he states, even if it had occurred. You have viewed these premises yourselves, and I feel well satisfied that the result of that view was to impress your minds with the belief that these witnesses have been guilty of perjury; that these defendants did not vainly boast they could get men who would swear for them at any time.

I think gentlemen, I might now safely leave this branch of the case; but there are one or two other ear marks of falsehood, so plain that although loathe to trespass on your time, I cannot pass them by. You will notice that these four witnsesses came from different directions to nearly the same spot, and at the same time; and although they each claim to have had peculiar business there, the moment they see what they have testified to, the *business* is forgotten and abandoned. Thus, old Beeman quit his work to find his son; he saw the man get out of the buggy, did'nt think it strange, yet although the son stood in plain view, within twenty rods of him, he walked straight back to his work, and looked no farther. Young Beeman went to see if there were cattle in the field, but the moment he saw the buggy he forgot his business, and wanted to see the man safely into the field, and then went to the house. Secord came down from the distilery, over a mile to look for a beetle and wedge; he did'nt find it; but he saw the man get out of the buggy and we hear no more of the beetle and wedge. Taylor goes from home in search of a boy; goes round by the mill to see if he can find Zeikle's boy; hears Zeikle himself is likely to be from home; meets a man with a bundle and passes Zeikle's door; never stops to inquire about the boy, and never gets one after. Surely this might be enough; but there is still another sign. You will remember gentlemen, that in his opening speech on the 8th day of July, the counsel for defence told you they would prove that on that day Lake and Phelps came along south of Leoni, with the box in a red handkerchief; that Lake got out, put it under his arm, and went across the fields towards the Centre; now the question is from whom had counsel learned these *facts?* Not from Secord, for on the 22d July he tells you, "I did not know for certain till I was subpœned yesterday, that I would be a witness." And again he says:

"When Bennet spoke to me on Sunday, it did not occur to me, that about the men in the wagon would be important; never did before Sunday; don't know that it ever occurred to me that about the wagon would be important." Nor from old Beeman, for on August 5th, he says:—

"I came here yesterday; was subpœned on Monday by Cozier.—Last Saturday Higby asked me what I had seen, and I told him, and that was the first time I ever told any one what I had seen."

Nor from young Beeman, for on August 5th, he says he saw Bennett and Cozier on Wednesday. "When I saw Bennett and Cozier was the first I told of what I saw."

Nor from Taylor, for on August the 9th, he tells you he was subpœned a few days before, and until then, never told what he saw; or said any thing about it, but to once ask young Beeman if he saw such a man, when B. replied he did'nt recollect seeing him. It is clear then that the information did'nt come from any witness produced on the stand. How did it come. Was counsel told he might go on and state it boldly, that the proof would be forth coming? It looks like this, for it was just the place and incident to be selected for a successful perjury. Before leaving this subject, I must call your attention to a mark of falsity in a witness which is laid down in the books—1 Starkie, p. 547—laying down several indications of insincerity in a witness, says "an affectation of indifference, are all to a greater or lesser extent, obvious marks of insincerity." Apply this rule to these witnesses; old Beeman says he never spoke of what he saw, to avoid being a witness; yet one of the defendants is married to his niece. Young Beeman never spoke of it for the same reason; and Taylor, when the constable first asked him, denied having seen the man, and only acknowledged it when he was subpœned, and found he had to come. Add to this, gentlemen, the absurd improbability, that in seeking secrecy, Lake would take the box out of the buggy, and carry it four miles under his arm, along a public highway, and then ask yourselves what marks of falsehood does this testimony lack. It is improbable—the witnesses contradict themselves, and contradict each other; they are contradicted in material points; no account is given how their evidence got to the knowledge of the defenee. Although the most important witnesses for the defence, if true, they are not subpœned till almost its close; although speaking to one point, they straggle in, one now, and one again, over a space of some 17 days. It was just at the commencement of these delays, of which so much has been said, that these witnesses were subpœned. Sum up all of these circumstances, gentlemen, and tell me how you can avoid the conviction that these witnesses are false? or upon what grounds you can give the slightest credence to a word they uttered.

Although not directly connected with the narrtive of Phelps, I may in this connection dispose of the testimony of Arnold. You will remember he was called to prove that Lake had a bundle, in a red handkerchief of course, at Filley's on the afternoon of the 11th April.—That was the single point that he was to swear to, and when he passed beyond that he contradicted himself in every sentence. If I could feel assured that you remembered his appearance on the stand, I would dismiss him without a single word, but lest you should not, I will read to you some portions of his evidence which are characteristic of the entire, and will serve to refresh your memories in relation to him.

(Heie counsel read from the tstimony of Arnold.)

You perceive that four or five times he repeats that whatever day he saw Lake, he went to Quigley's at Brooklyn, the second day after.—He can't be mistaken about this. He gives a statement of how he was employed the day he saw Lake, what he worked at the next day, and *is certain* the third day he went to Brooklyn and stayed over night at Quigley's. But unfortunately for the reputation of Mr. Arnold, Quigley and Miss Ellen Quigley have a distinct recollection of the only occasion when he stayed over night at their house, and swear positively it was on the 18th of April. They cannot be mistaken for besides other reasons for remembering, they remarked the next day on hearing that all the people at the Centre were arrested, that Arnold was *not*, for he was at their house the night of the arrests, which was the night of the 18th, or the morning of the 19th. You will notice that he swears by the entries in his account book, yet like Bildad Bennett's docket, the account book is not here, it may be good enough to *swear by*, but not good enough for inspection. Produced, however, we are fortunately able to gather some idea of its *accuracy* from the following portion of his testimony. You will remember that Sunday was the 3d of the month. He says:

" Can write and keep my own books, looked last at the book on Sunday, made a charge there last Sunday, with the dates, it does not concern this case what dates—the dates I put down were the 3d, 4th and 5th of this month, it was Monday I made the charges. Mis-spoke when I said the 5th—I made a charge for the 5th—worked for Laycock on the 3d and 4th—worked for him on Sunday—now you have it.

Unless aided in your memory this testimony gives but an imperfect idea of his accuracy; you will recollect that his 3d, 4th and 5th came out only as he was each time laughingly reminded that he was still making entries in advance, and he was so ready and willing to change the date of his entry, that a sober face, might have led him on to the twentieth, perhaps the *fiftieth* of the month. I leave Mr. Arnold. I know that when he left the stand you did not believe a word he uttered,and I know his credibility is not much strengthened by association, of being a witness to the same point with the Beemans.

Phelps states that on the evening of the 11th he was again at Coykendalls, that Myers and Corwin went with him from there to the Centre. These, the leading and material facts of this testimony, are corroborated by the witnesses for the defence; but it is sought to establish a contradiction by Coykendall, who swears that Phelps paid for twenty cents' worth of liquor, that was carried by them to the Centre. Kellogg and Smith also prove that they saw him pay for liquor, but their evidence amounts to nothing, as Phelps himself admits that he treated several times and paid. Coykendall is the only one who swears he paid for the liquor that was carried away. Apart from its bearing on the truthfulness of Phelps, it is entirely immaterial who paid for the liquor; and if Phelps paid, why should he deny it? But to set the whole matter at rest, Phelps says Corwin paid for it; and at page 155 Falkner says Corwin asked Fitch to drink out of the jug, and adds, "Corwin told him he need not fear it, as he had paid for it."

The next portion of Phelp's testimony is a detail of the conversation and occurrences at the Centre on the night of the 11th April,when the match was delivered to burn the depot at Niles. As this portion of the case is important, and if true stamps the impress of guilt upon many of the defendants, I will detain you by reading a portion of it. After stating that he, Myers and Corwin arrived at the Centre, he proceeds at page. 139, as follows:

"Arrived after dark, and stopped at Filley's hotel, found Mr. Falkner there. Soon after we got there, H. Hay, and Lake came in, and soon after Fitch came, and by and by Wm. Hudson, came in: don't remember any one else. Fitch took me on one side and said Filley had told him that if I was going to Niles at all, I was going that evening. I told him that was my object in coming there; he said a lot of fellows had been hanging around there, and he had sent Filley off with them fishing. I asked him for some money, he said he would not pay us anything more until after we returned, but if we succeeded in burning the depot, we might come back and take the oxen, and they would pay over the balance of $60. I know Corwin, Myers, and Falkner were in hearing of part of this talk; I spoke loud, told them I wanted them to be ready to pay me when I got back, that I was going to Minnesota; Fitch, Corwin and Lake went out of doors together, and Fitch said to Lake and me that he supposed we knew the consequences of bad faith towards them—that if we made any exposures we had better dig our graves before we went; then said he would give us a match all ready, which if we once got inside of the depot there would be no difficulty about it; said we should have to get some turpentine or camphene, and put it into the box out there, as we could not well carry it with us, said our best way was to take it in our buggy and go back to Grass Lake, and one stay there and the other go farther east and get on the morning train at different places; said the match was on the same principle as the one he had furnished Gay with, and it would not fail, as they had tried it several times; went into the house again and spoke of money, I wanted some in advance, and Corwin gave me fifty cents, saying that would help to pay for drink on the road anyhow.

A remark was made in the room that if we were successful in this and other plans they would be able to make a raise out of the company. Fitch said if you are successful, when you come back we will go to Kirkendall's and have a bust; Corwin said yes, we will tear his bar down. When we spoke of money, Fitch said it would be ready when I came back from Niles; that he had plenty of it that was not yet galvanized, but would be before I got back, and I could have plenty of it; that they would be flush when I got back.

Something was said about my claim before the Legislature; Fitch wanted to know how I got along with it; I told him I should probably get about $3,000. Fitch said to Corwin we had better fix them off before Filley gets back with the men fishing. Corwin went to a small room, unlocked it, and brought out the match under his arm, and placed it in the buggy, and said there, boys, it's all right; as he went out with the box nearly all hands started to follow; I got up and shut the door, and told them they could not go out; they then went out by the north door; Fitch went away before, after telling Corwin to go and get the box."

It is claimed by the defence that the testimony of Amanda Fitch, Mr. Cross and Mr. Hudson, precludes the possibility of Fitch having been at Filley's on that night, for the length of time impled by Phelps. A very few words will dispose of this objection. As usual, when Phelps is sought to be contradicted, the witnesses begin by corroborating him. In this instance, they all prove his presence there that night, but differ from Phelps, Faulkner, Lake, and each other, as to the time he remained there. Thus Amanda Fitch says he was not absent from his house over five or ten minutes—Mr. Cross says 8 or 10 minutes, and by turning to Mr. Hudson's testimony, you will perceive he makes it over half an hour, for he says he found Fitch standing outside, went in and Fitch followed him. There was then some drinking, after which Fitch and Filley talked some 10 or 15 minutes. After this he says he *did not see* Fitch, but he does not know when he left. But the accuracy of this witness cannot be at all relied on, for though he remained till all left he never saw the box. I will hereafter show you that Hudson corroborates Phelps in many essential particulars, but for the present pass from this branch of the case as in connection with the testimony of Faulkner, I will show you how unerringly the occurrences of this evening indicate the guilt of the defendants—how fully Phelps is corroborated, and the impossibility of his evidence in this regard being untrue. I will also for the present pass over the evidence of Phelps in relation to his interview with Filley at Jackson; in another connection I will refer to its corroboration and show its important bearing in the case, and will now briefly call your attention to other grounds of discredit urged against this witness.—

Reference has been made to his *demeanor* on the stand and his conduct in reference to the jury and counsel.

Surely the phillipic indulged in by the learned counsel in this respect, must have been an after-thought, and part and parcel of elaborate *preparation.* I cannot but think that *at the time,* the testimony was given, he must have been favorably impressed, as doubtless you were, with the bearing of the witness. Examined at great length and thro' vast detail, tortured by a cross examination through several days with great ability and severity on the part of the learned counsel, he yet held the even tenor of his way, calm, prompt, and frank, thoughtful but not reluctant; willing but not forward; never volunteering, but always responsive, he stood through the long ordeal, and came out not only unhurt, but I submit to you, with his whole story strengthened by the severe test which failed to shake it.

But, says the counsel, he impudently assailed William Dyer, a respectable citizen of Indiana, and denounced him as the identical horse thief Lozier. Most singular thing for this defence to revive!

You recollect the scene. Hawley had just poured out his afterwards recanted perjuries on the head of Phelps. Phelps was again put on the stand by the defence to lay the foundation for new impeachments.

"Did you not so tell William Dyer, of Indiana?" &c. "I don't know him," said Phelps, "produce him and I will say if I ever even saw him." And in came William Dyer, stealing with trembling paces over the floor. Phelps fixes his eye upon him, and declares his belief that it was Lozier the horse thief. Gentlemen, is this a circumstance against Phelps? Would he thus have denounced the man, if he had not believed he spoke the truth, when he knew, if untrue, fifty witnesses could be brought to contradict him? Gentlemen, he may have been mistaken in the name of Dyer, but not in much else. He sent to Indiana for witnessess to meet this William Dyer. Hawley was arrested—Dyer was about to be; he fled from the State, the "respectable citizen of Indiana" returned to his native tamarack and his miserabl testimony was stricken in disgust from the case.

But Phelps is charged to have on several occasions intruded himself offensively on this Jury. I appeal to you if this is true. Has he not, on the contrary, invariably been reserved, kept himself aloof, and behaved so modestly as to have attracted your observation and gained your approval? Aye, but he sat here at the head of counsel for the Prosecution, "*observing* their course." Withering remark! Bitter sarcasm! I saw my leaaned associates took it very quietly, showed no "visible sign," but bore it as philosophically as if they had sat at the bar before, and with others, which made it quite as humiliating as when *headed* by Henry Phelps.

And all this tirade poured out on this bar because on an attempt being made to impeach Phelps, he was permitted, according to invariable custom, to sit by counsel and suggest what might be useful in process of examination!

Time will not permit me, nor does my own sense of duty prompt to pursue this further. The learned counsel strikes at both friend and foe, and for the sake of a hit at Phelps, would even sacrifice his own colleague. One *would* have supposed that in view of all that *was* proved and offered to be proved, *one thing* would have been permitted to sleep. I will not for a petty triumph inflict a blow on one whose own associate would not spare him.

You have seen Phelps from day to day, his incomings and outgoings, his patience, candor, and gentleness. You have seen the storm of hatred poured down upon his head. You have seen Hawley and Dyer conjured up from swamp and morass, and kindred spirits in swarms gather to destroy him. All that malice could suggest, all that ingenuity could devise, all that perjury could execute, was done. He stood still; the storm passed; and Phelps and his testimony remained unhurt amidst all this "war of elements."

But it is said his story is not probable; that Fitch had no motive to engage in such crimes; that these defendants are too humble, obscure and few, to have attempted such acts against a powerful company; that most of them were poor and could not have contributed to a fund for burning Depots; that Phelps stands a self-acknowledged liar, because he made false pretences as to his mission among them, and that other improbabilities exist, which I dare not detain you to even call up for investigation.

How these and all the other improbabilities suggested in the story of Phelps disappear on a little reflection.

These men were *not* weak but strong, constituting a very considable portion of the town of Leoni; strong in hatred of the Railroad; strong in their union against it; strong in their criminal successes; strong in all the elements of a dire and fearful conspiracy; each one could readily procure the respective amounts which they are alleged to have contributed for the arson of the Depot, and each one had fierce desire enough for its destruction to sacaifice his last coin to reward the incendiary.

How weak to talk of want of motive in Fitch to be participiant or adviser in such offences, when he is found through years denouncing this Road, uttering bitter maledictions against it, justifying every outrage upon it; when he carried around with him through the long day and the quiet night the spirit of undying revenge, which haunted him to the last? How futile to denounce Phelps because he did not unfold to these prisoners the true object of his action, and defeat at once every chance of developing the deep seated wickedness of Leoni?

The story, gentlemen, is natural and probable all over. Not only is it corroborated, consistent and inherently true, but most *probable* in every aspect. It is probable, as being the almost necessary result of the threats, conduct and combination of defendants.

They had determined on vengeance; they had entered on a wild career of crime and recklessness. They had set the laws at defiance; brought themselves to believe in the corruption of Courts and the unmitigated depravity of all mankind. They had abandoned the sweets of domestic bliss, and the repose of rural life. Their Sabbaths were desecrated; their nights consumed in revels; visions of fiendish violence perpetually flitted across their minds, and details of their execution furnished the richest enjoyment.

Gentlemen, all this, and far more than all this, does the testimony in this case tell us. I will not enlarge upon the theme, but with your permission I will read to you a page of moral philosophy by an eminent writer, which may furnish some food for reflection, and perhaps strike you as having some application to the case before you.

["The man who habitually violates his conscience, not only is more feebly impelled to do right, but he becomes less sensible to the pain of doing wrong. A child feels poignant remorse after the first act of pilfering. Let the habit of dishonesty be formed, and he will be come so hackneyed in sin, that he will perpetrate robbery with no other feeling than that of mere fear of detection. The first oath almost palsies the tongue of the stripling. It requires but a few months, however, to transform him into the bold and thoughtless blasphemer. The murderer, after the death of his first victim, is agitated with all the horrors of guilt. He may, however, pursue his trade of blood, until he have no more feeling for man, than the butcher for the animal which he slaughters. Burke, who was in the habit of murdering men for the purpose of selling their bodies to the surgeons for dissection, confessed this of himself. Nor is this true of individuals alone. *Whole communities may become so accustomed to deeds of violence*, as not merely to loose all the milder sympathies of their nature, but also to take pleasure in exhibitions of the most revolting ferocity. Such was the case in Rome at the period of the Gladiatorial contests; and such was the fact in Paris, at the time of the French revolution.

This also serves to illustrate a frequently repeated aphorism: *Guem deus vrelt perdere prius demental.* As a man becomes more wicked, he becomes bolder in crime. Unchecked by conscience, he ventures upon more and more atrocious villainy, and he does it with less and less precaution. As, in the earliest stages of guilt he is betrayed by timidity, in the latter stages of it he is exposed by his recklessness. He is thus discovered by the very effect which his conduct is producing upon his own mind.

Thus we see, that by every step in our progress in virtue, the succeeding step becomes less difficult. In proportion as we deny our passions, they become less imperative. The oftener we conquer them, the less is the moral effort necessary to secure the victory, and the less frequently and the less powerfully do they assail us. By every art of successful resistance, we diminish the tremendous power of habit over us, and thus become more perfectly under the government of our own will. Thus, with every act of obedience to conscience, our character is fixed upon a more immoveable foundation.

And, on the contrary, by every act of vicious indulgence, we give our passions more uncontrolled power over us, and diminish the power of reason and of conscience. Thus, by every act of sin, we not only incur new guilt, but we strengthen the bias towards sin, during the whole of our subsequent being."

Gentlemen, I have shown you how wonderfully corroborated is this testimony of Phelps. It does not rest upon him for its truth, even if we conceded his untruthfulness. His evidence in this case stands so fortified, so necessarily true by reason of the corroborations, it is so full of consistencies, that we must still believe it. Speaking of the power and effect of such consistencies and corroborations, Starkie remarks: "So far does the principle extend, that in many cases, except for the purpose of repelling suspicion of fraud and concert, the credit of the witness himself for honesty and verity, may become wholly immaterial."

I have heretofore noted the vast detail and variety of circumstances which the testimony of Phelps includes and goes over. The Court will instruct you that it is one of the great ear-marks of a truthful witness; keeping nothing back; disclosing every pertinent thing; and affording to the adverse party every opportunity of following in his footsteps, and detecting his errors; "affording a wide field for contradiction, if his testimony be false."]

I have heretofore pointed out to you, in canvassing his testimony before you, many of the inherent evidences of truth which it contains. I now beg to submit if it is probable, nay, if it is possible, for living man to have fabricated such a story; to fill it with details, dates, time, space, and circumstances; changing from point to point, and embracing such a variety of persons and incidents; to cling to it through every effort to disturb him; and come out from it as uncontradicted as this man does. If truthful, he might narrate and renarrate the simple truth, and never vary; but if false, I hold that it would be a moral impossibility.

I submit to you, gentlemen, that the story of Phelps is natural, probable, consistent, corroborated; unlikely, if not impossible to be false, under all the circumstances; and is stamped with every evidence of truth, the whole truth, and nothing but the truth.

Gentlemen, having thus passed over Phelps and his evidence, save as to the two points yet remaining to be hereafter noticed, I turn to Lake, and his. I will not consume much of your time on this branch of the case. If I have succeeded in establishing before you the fact, that Phelps' evidence, in all material respects, is in the law and in reason entitled to credence, then it is useless to travel over that of Lake in detail; for as far as it goes, it is substantially the same as Phelps; is corroboroted by the same or similar circumstances and witnesses; contains many of the same inherent marks of truth; is equally consistent and probable; and in some of its features has not even the grounds of suspicion which counsel supposed they detected in the other.

Lake is still a young man. True, he too has been to State's Prison; but not for an offense which even at common law would have rendered him infamous, or barred him from testifying in a court of justice. He was convicted for procuring to be carried into a county jail, a file to aid a friend in making his escape. It was a violation of law; it deserved punishment, and he received it. But I submit to you that such an act, and especially done by a mere youth, as he then was, in behalf of an imprisoned friend, does not necessarily evince a bad heart; nor does it in law or morals constitute any reason for doubting his truth, or refusing him credence. He has lived long in the State, yet there is no impeachment against him. He is not successfully or materially contradicted; and but one fact has transpired to justify us in suspecting his morals, and that but in one respect, and not pertaining to the truth of his story here.

He and Phelps in States Prison; they were not partlcularly friendly there, indeed at times were inimical. You recollect, and I will not detain you to rehearse, the accidental meeting between himself and Phelps after both were released from Prison; and the circumstances under which Lake became engaged in the service of the Rail Road.

I *will* recall to your minds his demeanor on the stand before you. I appeal to you if it was not prepossessing, frank, and kindly. He answered fully to direct and cross examination; gave details at length and appeared to be neither moved by prejudice, or warmed by zeal against these prisoners.

Why should Heman Lake not be believed? The learned counsel for the prisoners amused himself through a four months labor, by picking out and serving up for your benefit, various little differences between the narrative of Phelps and Lake; and says, that when present at interview with some of these defendants Lake details some incident, remark, or fact additional to that related by Phelps, or *vice versa;* that he sometimes ascribes a remark to one defendant when Phelps puts it in the mouth of a different one &c.

Gentlemen, we are not engaged in children's play, but in a serious struggle in the battle of life. Grown up, intelligent and experienced men, are not by such means to have their minds diverted from the truth. You need not to be told that different persons will narrate different facts, and words, and scenes, in different language; that one will forget, or remember a distinct fact which another may not; that one hears or observes what another does not. Opportunity, strength of memory, power of observation, distinctness of vision; a large variety of circumstances, all tend to produce a variety of descriptions of the same thing, from a variety of narrators, and yet the tales of all will be substantially true. In the language of Starkie, "it is to be observed that partial variances in the testimony of different witness, on minute or collateral points although they frequently afford the adverse advocate a topic for *copious observation*, are of little importance unless they be of too prominent and striking a nature to be ascribed to inadvertence inattention or defect of memory;" and he might have added further to the list.

Apply this principle to the alleged variances between Phelps and Lake, and it covers nearly the whole of them. Nay, gentlemen, I submit, that the alleged differences strengthen the testimony of these witnesses, for they repel the idea of concert, and show that each gave "the substantial truth under circumstantial variety," just as it occurred to their memories without practicing to swear alike.

But the Counsel tells you Lake swears that in arriving at Filley's they enquired of him if "the boys" were there, although according to his version he and Phelps had just passed Leoni where "the boys lived." The answer is ready. Only a few of "the boys" lived at the village of Leoni; and again, Phelps and Lake, both claim to have passed not through Leoni, but by a different route, and hence the greater the pertinency and likelihood of the enquiry for "the boys."

But we have some more grave objections. Counsel tells us that Lake's statement as to the interview with Filley when he arrived there on the 11th of April is false, and unfortunate for his truth, because Kane and Allen, who came down to sport, took Filley off to the pond, about half past twelve, before Lake came, and kept him there till between 3 and 4 o'clock P. M.

This presents no difficulty. Turn to the testimony. Phelps and Lake got to Filley's about noon. Phelps drove off; Lake "got something to eat, and being sick soon went to bed." Soon after, Kane and Allen came, took their dinner, and went off with Filley; no discrepancy whatever; and Lake himself testifies to the fact that they were there.

But Lake blaims he only slept an hour, and came down and renewed his talk with Filley, when in fact Filley was off at the pond.

It is not likely that Lake, who it is conceded was there that afternoon, would locate an interview with Filley when he was absent; knowing it could be readily disproved. It is far more likely that an interview did occur, but at a later hour; that Lake worn out with fatigue, and weak with the remains of sickness, sank into a deep sleep, which lasted much longer than he then supposed or now recollect.

But counsel tell us that if he was sick before, he must, like Don Juan, in the ship-wreck have "fallen sicker" to have thus enlarged his repose.

Oh! What a fall was there my countrymen, from the classic and chaste reading of the virtuous Addison, clear down to the forbidden pages of Don Juan! I feared the learned counsel, having given us a slight specimen of his light readings, was about to continue with the ejaculation of the sea-sick lover till he would have to exclaim with his hero as he grew sicker,

> "For God's sake let me have a little liquor,
> Pedro Baptisto, help me down below."

Gentlemen, I leave such trifling and return to Lake. The hour of adjournment has about come, and I will not pursue his alleged contradictions. Several of those against him, have already been answered in the course of this argument in reference to Phelps, and as to anything which may remain, you will find if it is deemed necessary to pursue them, that they can be quite as readily disposed of as those I have already refered to.

The corroborations of his testimony are as palpable, thick and convincing, as in the case of Phelps, and all the reasons why he should be believed, arising from consistency, demeanor, corroborations, probability, detail and inherent truth of his story, which were urged on the argument as to Phelps, here exist and might be again repeated. He had no revenge to gratify against a single defendant. He is still in early manhood, with feelings apparently fresh and kindly. No motive to perjure himself is suggested, and I insist that no man without more years, more experience, education shrewdness and talent than Heman Lake possesses, could have woven such a tale, or adopted it from the rehearsal of another, adhere to it with such exactness, giving in dates, time, place and circumstances, and cling to his story through such a cross-examination, come out from it unscathed and remain to the end so uncontradicted, unless on the hypothesis that it was the truth he narrated and adhered to. Had it been a mere fabrication, confusion, contradiction and disgrace would have marked its progress and overwhelmed its author.

I leave him with you: you will understand, that fear of trespassing on your kind attention, alone, prevents me from more fully vindicating his evidence, and refuting the assault made upon it. I feel it is not necessary, nor will I stop to give an analysis of what he testified to before you. Suffice it to say, that he mingled with these defendants freely, was trusted and relied upon by them; that they freely conversed and unbosomed themselves to him; that they deemed him a member of their conspiracy; an agent to effect and consummate their vengeancee, and he was hallowed in their sight by supposed maturity in crime.

Thus familiar with them, their thoughts, feelings, designs and deeds, he confirms to you all others have said of their deadly malice against the Railroad company; of frequent depredations against their rights; of fearful obstructions on their track, and of a deep determination to continue on their lawless course, until they brought the company to terms. He swears to you distinctly that part of these defendants, whom he names, had contributed to the burning of the depot in Detroit—rejoiced over its destruction, and were intending, and devising ere long to gloat their vengeance with new fires, and continous destruction, of every depot along the line of the road.

I will not trouble you furtber to-day. To-morrow morning I will briefly refer to the meeting between Phelps and Ami Filley at Jackson, after the attempt to burn the Niles depot, testified to by Van Arman, Clark, Spaulding, and Phelps; to the testimony of Faulkner, and to the declarations by several of these defendants on board of the cars after the arrest, as proven by Dr. Hahan and others. I will then point out more distinctly than has yet been done those of these defendants who stand identified with the overt act, charged in the indictment, and, having done this, I will hurry on to the close and leave the rest with you.

(In consequence of the temporary illness of one of the Jurors, the Court adjourned from day to day, until Thursday, Sep., 25th, when, the Court being in session, Mr. Van Dyke continued his argument as follows):

Gentlemen :—I cannot refrain from expressing my gratitude on this beautiful morning, at seeing Court and Jury before me, all again in the enjoyment of reasonable health and vigor—prepared to go through with what yet remains of this protracted trial. But especially must it cheer you, as it does me, that there is every probability of to-morrow's morn finding us free from all these labors, responsibilities, and cares, to breathe fresh, unburthened by them.— I announced to you, at our last adjournment, the few points which I deemed it proper to yet call up and discuss before you. I will proceed to them at once, but before doing so beg to briefly call to your minds that portion of the case and argument already gone through. (Here counsel reviewed briefly his previous argument, and continued):

You of course recollect the scene at Filley's bar-room, on the evening of April 11th, as described by Phelps and Lake. The importance of the testimany on this point is manifest, as it affects the whole case. If true, it must go far to lead your minds to a conclusion; for it tends to show that Wescott testified truly when he told you, that burning depots was within the scope and extent of the conspiracy. It proves the *modns operandi*: a match in possession of defendants to accomplish the arson, and thus links that material fact with the matches at Gay's and his use of them. It corroborates powerfully Phelps and Lake, confirms the theory of this prosecution and connects and identifies part of these defendrnts with the continnous carrying into effect of that conspiracy, of which the arson of the Detroit Depot was merely an earlier step.

The learned counsel for the defence passed this part of the case over lightly; suggested that Faulkner was a stranger, and probably confused, and that the whole affair was of but little moment.

But one theory is given us by the defence, to account for the facts testified to by Faulkner, viz:—That *there was* a scheme of wickedness set on foot there that night; that Phelps and Lake were being fitted out on a "bogus" expedition. I will go over this point with sufficient care, and feel free to say to you, and believe you will soon agree with me, that it is one of fatal force against this defence; that their theory wholly fails to account for the facts which occurred: but that that they are reconcilable with the theory of the prosecution, and with none other.

And first: Who is John Faulkner? You observed him on the stand—modest, respectful. and intellgent; his appearance striking every beholder most favorably; his recollection apparently so distinct; his memory so clear; his whole demeanor free from confusion, and enforcing the simple narrative he gave on every candid mind. He is a resident of the beautiful village of Marshall, where he has resided for years, and where, as you are assured, he has received, by his course of conduct, the good will of his fellow citizens and a reputation beyond his station in life.

I need not tell you, that he is here wholly unimpeached, contradicted, and unquestioned; even counsel on the other side, have had to admit his honesty. Thus stands John Faulkner before you. And you will bear in mind, too, that, up to the night he speaks of, he had no acquaintance with Phelps or Lake. Now hear his story, which I must give you in his own words, and at some length.

"I reside at Marshall; been there seven years; am a cartman; remember on the 11th April last, going to Michigan Centre; left

Marshall on the cars, got off at Grass Lake, and went back to the Centre on foot; at Grass Laee saw Mr. Clark, the only man I knew; I had an axe and small budget with me; when I arrived at the Centre I stopped at Ami Filley's tavern ; Filley was not there ; Mrs. F., and a girl they called Bridget, and a boy and a Mr. Lockwood were there; L. soon left. I asked for supper and lodging; while at supper, Phelps, Lake, and a man they called Wm. Corwin, and Daniel Myers came into the bar-room ; found them there when I went out.

When I first went into the bar-room they were talking low together ; could only once in a while hear a word ; heard these words from Corwin, "yes after we pet through:" and " think we can come it." After they got through they went to the fire-place, and Phelps said loudly, "boys, when I get back from Niles, we will have a time." Corwin replied, "yes, we will, we will tear down Kirkeneall's bar, and this too;" something was said about pay; Corwin said, "I am willing to pay something in advance," and took out his wallet and gave him something. Phelps remarked, "this will help pay expenses over the road, all paid in advance helps like hell."

They continued to talk, and went out doors, and soon after came back with two others, whom they called Hudson and " Hi. Hay." They talked privately; soon a man came in they called " Capt. Fitch;" it is the same one here now ; he said, "boys, how do you do?" and shook hands with Phelps; asked what's the news. Phelps replied, about as usual. He then went round from one to another asking, "what's the news." He asked Bill Corwin three several times, "what's the news?" they all went out doors, were gone about five minutes and came in again; Phelps and Capt. Fitch stood by the counter alone; the rest sat down on a bench. Heard Fitch say to Phelps, "*when you get back I shall be ready, I shall be flush then.*" Before Fitch came in, Corwin said it should be right, and money would be flush ; this was the time when Phelps spoke of when he would get back from Niles.

Soon after, they all went out again, and I moved the light from the bar counter to the mantle-piece; Corwin, Phelps, Hay and Hudson, or Myers, came in agsin in a short time; Corwin unlocked a door leading to a small room, and went in the dark, he brought out a small box, five or six by ten or twelve inches in size; in locking the door he *had to use both hands, and the box slid down, but he caught it before it struck the floor*, he then locked the door and put the key in his pocket ; Corwin then passed out doors with the box, and Phelps got up and shut the outside door and put his back against it, saying no one could go out, the others tnen went out a side door, and Phelps then opened the one he was holding, anb went out and left it open; I looked out and saw Corwin and Myers under a shed near; very soon they came from the shed and put the small box Corwin carried out under the seat in a one horse wagon standing near by; Lake came from the shed also; Corwin went to another wagon, and untied the horse ; Lake went to the wagon where the box was, and called Corwin, and asked is "that all right?" Corwin answered "yes." Lake and Phelps got into one wagon, and Corwin and Myers into the other, and they droue off, that was the last I saw of them, they were about there some two hours; I saw nothing else put into the wagon; saw a jug of whiskey, but don't know what was done with it.

They asked Capt. Fitch to drink, but he refused, saying it gave him a pain in the side. Corwin told him he need not fear it, as he had paid for it. *Fitch stood on the opposite side of the wagon when they put the box in.* There was something said about going to Lansing. When they talked, they generally stood close together, and spoke low, so I only heard a part of the conversation."

[Here a box containing the match placed in the Niles Depot, was exhibited to the witneness, and he recognized it as the one, or exactly similar to the one Corwin took out of the room and put in the wagon.]

"I saw the same box the next day at Bank's office in Marshall."

Gentlemen, it *is* true then, that Phelps and Lake, Fitch, Corwin and the others alluded to above, were at the bar-room of Ammi Filley on the night of the 11th of April last. It *is* true that something peculiar and unusual did occur, and that private conversations took place between the actors. The expedition was being fitted out *for Niles*, to be performed by Phelps, and on his return, he was to be paid for his exploits, which were to be celebrated by tearing down Kirkendall's bar.

To a remark of Phelps, Corwin says "yes after we get through," and he was "willing to pay something in advance." And Fitch says "yes, when *you get back*, I shall be flush then."

You observe too, that Corwin brought the box from the small room, and was it placed as described in the buggy of Phelps and Lake, who were afterwards sent on their way.

Now, what is said of this strange scene? Is it met fairly and overcome, or is it sought to be avoided by sophistry? If the latter, it only stands out the more prominent, as not being capable of explanation or disproof on the theory or evidence of the defence.

It was suggested on argument that it was a bogus expedition—a joint operation to circulate false and counterfeit money. See the inconsistencies to which erroneous theories are driven. This defence tells us at another time, that it is ridiculous to suppose that Capt. Fitch would have anything to do with "bogus money," and that all the search of the police never found a vestige of it, or of implements to make it, about the premises of any of the defendants. But if filled with counterfeit coin, could Corwin have carried such a box, thus weighty, under one arm, use both hands to lock the door and catch the box as it slid down, before it struck the floor? If only partially filled, would not the rattle and noise of the box thus sliding down and caught, have attracted the notice of the attentive Faulkner? And as to counterfeit bank bills, it occurs to you at once that it would be an unlikely mode to be selected for conveying them through the country for circulation. But on this theory, why was Phelps to *be paid* on his return? Would *he* not rather haveo divide the spoils with *them?* Why was his return to be the cause of so much rejoicing? Why was Niles *alone* mentioned as the place of his proposed action? You see gentlemen, that the whole transaction, everything said and done, is inconsistent with the attempted explanation. The learned counsel, who last addressed you, says that Faulkner was a stranger; confounded one with another, and heard only a "suppressed conversation." Faulkner *was* a stranger, but exhibits no likelihood of confusion. He was too cool, too observant, too intelligent, to have confounded one with another. He shows no sign of it here. He swears distinctly, and designates in open Court, without mistake or "confusion" the actors of that evening. True he did not hear all the conversation, but he saw all that transpired, and heard enough to render his narrative clear, and free from all ambiguity. The sentences he does give, are perfect in themselves and of convincing import.

But counsel say, Phelps was playing a part, "that he spoke aloud, only occasionally, when he desired a catchword to reach Faulkners ear." Faulkner only gives one instance of Phelps' speaking loudly, and he tells you he heard the expressions from Corwin and Fitch with perfect distinctness, and which of course Phelps could not have produced as cues or catchwords.

But it is further objected that it is manifest that Faulkner is mistaken in supposing Fitch spoke of "being flush" on Phelps return, because if heard by him they would also have been by Hudson who swears he did not hear them. Sulely this is a *non sequitur*. In the language of Starkie on evidence. "If one witness was positively to swear he saw or heard a fact, and another were merely to swear he was present, but did not hear or see, and the witnesses were equally faithworthy, the general principle would in ordinary cases create a preponderance in favor of the affirmative." But again, you will recollect that Hudson was a most inattentive observer. He says "I do not pretend to speak accurately as to time," does not know when Fitch left the room; he did not see even the box, although he says, one of the defendants, (Hiram Hay,) on the way home, "spoke of their having a box." Hudson confirms several of the expressions, and circumstances testified to by Faulkner, and contradicts none of his statements. He merely did *not* see, or did *not* hear.

Again, counsel say, Fitch had left the party and returned home, before the box was placed in the waggon, and therefore Faulkner is mistaken in sayiug he stood on the opposite side of the waggon on the occasion of putting in the box. Who proves this? If reference is had to the testimony of Cross and Amanda Fitch, I have examined it heretofore.

But it is said, that neither Lake, Phelps or Hudson pretend that Fitch was present at the place assigned him by Faulkner. Gentlemen, I will not delay to look at the evidence of Lake and Hudson, but turn to your book of evidence and on page 142 read the statement of Phelps. "I did not send Corwin to the small room to get the match; Fitch told him to do it, and *went and waited till we came out.* Something was said of words falling amid a drunken revel.

Fitch did *not drink,* " on account of a pain in his head." There is proof of drinking by others, and of anticipated revelry, when some deed of evil should be performed. There is no evidence that any one was drunk that evening. The counsel remarked that he saw nothing strange in Corwins speaking of a revel when Phelps should return laden with three thousand two hundred dollars from the State of Michigan ; or with moneys from Masachusetts ; or a fotune from Minesota.

What think ye of such a fair defence ? What reliance shall be placed on such " arguments ?" It was to *Niles,* Phelps was to go, *not* to Lansing, or Massachusetts, or Minnesota. It was from *Niles* he was to return. Then was the revel to be had ; then when gloating over the details of the burncd depot, and the trinmph of vengeance over the interests of the Rail Road, was Phelps to be crowned a Hero. and to be rewarded for his deeds.

I will not pursue this further. If the defence had any other theory to account for the transactions of that night, they were bound to present it, failing to do so, the narrative stands untouched.

" Error wounded writhes in pain,
And dies amid her worshipers."

I will not comment further on the force and effect of this startling evidence. There it stands, pressing this unfortunate defence on to its overthrow.

Gentlemen, Phelps and Lake proceeded to Niles. There they acted the part described by them. They returned to Jackson ; and Ami Filley, anxiously expectant, enquired of the result, heard of the failure to burn the depot, and invited Phelps to go to the Centre "and meet the boys." So says Phelps; and I submit this as fully corroborated, and proven by Van Arman, Clark and Spaulding. But says counsel, "it is a concerted corroboration;" the versions differ ; Van Arman heard only a part of that testified by Phelps ; Clark heard nothing.

Spaulding says, on the occasion referred to, "I saw Filley at the Jackson depot, waiting for the cars from the west; when they arrived Phelps stepped off, and Filley approached him, and talked *privately with him* while the cars stopped; Van Arman and Clark stood near, &c."

Mr. Van Arman testifies thus : "On the day Mr. Phelps returned from Niles, I came and got on the cars at Marshall ; found Phelps ; Clark was with me; we all came together to Jackson ; as soon as the cars stopped at Jackson, I saw a stranger approach the cars ; I have since learned that it was Mr. Ami Filley; Phelps told me so then. He met Phelps near the car, and talked ; I stood near where they were; heard Filley ask Phelps how he got along out there. Phelps' reply was low, and I did not hear it except the last of it, which was that it was a failure, and he didn't make more than nine times. There was other low talk, when P. spoke of leaving the cars, and Filley said P. had better go right down to the Centre, as the boys were there waiting for him. Phelps did not get on the cars again. Mr. Filley got on and rode to the Centre."

And Darius Clark, in speaking of the meeting at Jackson, after the firing of the Niles depot, testifies as follows: "I knew Ami Filley, at that time, and saw him and Phelps talking near the cars, after they stopped at Jackson; Van Arman was present; I came to Detroit: Filley went as far as the Centre; I saw several people there; Phelps stopped at Jackson; Filley's manner towards Phelps, when he met him at the cars, was cordial."

And yet these are the facts which are distorted into contradictions on the part of the witnesses detailing them. This is another instance of the perversion of the evidence *as it is*. There is in truth no contradiction whatever. Each detailed what he saw or heard. Filley would naturally speak fully and confidentially with Phelps; Van Arman, who was nearer than Clark, heard a few of the under sentences. Clark and Spaulding confirm the interview, the anxious waiting of Filley, and his cordial meeting with Phelps.

I will not say a word in reference to the attempt to throw suspicion, doubt or prejudice, over either of these witnesses. Attacks on them fall harmless, or recoil on the head of the aggressor. The poisoned arrows have failed to reach their intended victims. They stand observed, approved, and believed. If they have used extraordinary exertions and departed from mere ordinary rules, to ferret out this most extraordinary plot; if believing that there existed this fearful conspiracy which had violated the laws, disgraced the integrity of our State, rendered its highways mere avenues to death, and property mere objects for incendiary sport, and which yet bid defiance in its banded strength to detection and punishment; if these witnesses, believing all this, and that they had at last discovered the clue which would lead to its exposure, and yet were acutely vigilant, anxious and careful, before they struck the blow, to avoid rashness which might defeat justice or injure innocence; if it was thus they did, I submit they deserve well of their country; that every good citizen will yield them unceasing thanks; and that a refusal or a failure, to testify to what they alone could prove, would have been a weakness if not a crime.

And now, gentlemen, I must call your attention to another point which I promised to examine before you. It is briefly detailed by the witnesses who testify as to it; but I fear you cannot avoid finding in it, deep evidence of guilt. True, it only refers, in one portion of it, to a defendant who is no longer living; but *that* defendant was claimed by the prosecution as the "head and front of this offending;" and it was frequently averred by the defense, that he of all the others was the most unlikely to have had connection with or knowlgdge of Gay, or with these most heinous crimes.

I refer to the scene on the cars, the morning after the arrest of these prisoners, and I give you the language of the witnesses. Mr. Clark says: "I was present at the arrest of the defendants, and came in on the cars with them; saw Fitch. Warner asked who this Mr. Phelps was who made the complaint; said he did not know him; Fitch replied he did not know him neither. I saw Van Arman sitting with Fitch part of the time coming in."

Dr. James A. Hahn testifies: "I reside at Marshall; I was on the cars the morning of the arrest of some of the defendants; came down as far as Chelsea; saw Fitch, Tyrrell, Filley and Freeland aboard; heard a conversation between you [Van Arman] and Fitch; he asked you to see the warrant upon which he was arrested; you showed it to him, and he remarked, that he had a slight acquaintance with this Henry Phelps, some years ago, before he went to the State Prison; since then he had known but little about him. I think the conversation was voluntary on his part; did not hear you attempt to draw him out on any thing about the arrest. He said it appeared by the warrant, that he was implicated with a certain Mr. Gay, for burning the depot; said he never knew Gay, and never heard of him. He then paused a few moments, and again turned to you [Van Arman] and said, *I believe that old Gay has turued State's evidence;* I had not before heard of Gay, and did not know who it was; during that morning Freeland, G. Filley, and one other of defendants were sitting together in the cars talking; I heard them say that if they could get hold of that d——d Hank Phelps, they would make mince meat of him; that he had been with them all winter pretending to be a friend, and had now exposed the whole matter; I was sitting near them and overheard the whole talk; I pretended to be asleep during the time."

This evidence would seem not to need comment, but to speak for itself in a tone and with an import easily to be understood.

How is it replied to by the counsel, who surely must feel its importance? Observe how they would fain avoid matter of such serious moment. They say Clark must have been mistaken in his version of the words used by Fitch. But what a reason to advance to a jury! What right have you, in the face of evidence from a truthful witness, positive and distinct as it is, to presume any mistake or error? We must take it as true, because it is not disproved.

But observe again, the attempt to get rid of Dr. Hahn's testimony. The learned counsel last addressing you says, it amounts to nothing; if anything, Fitch's denial of knowledge of Gay is a contradiction of Phelps, as no one but Phelps testified to such knowledge; that the words about "old Gay turning State's evidence," were *suggested by his perusal of the warrant.* I give you as near as I can the words of the counsel on this point: "The counsel for the prosecution criticise the use of the word "old," which, they say, is inconsistent with Fitch's denial; but Fitch spoke of his knowledge of affairs before the arrest. After the arrest, "old Gay's" name must soon become familiar and common."

I confess, gentlemen, I do not perceive the force of this remark. Is this all the answer counsel could make? If so, it has not even the usual merit of sophistry.

Phelps had testified to admissions of Fitch that he knew Gay; Fitch is found denying it at one moment, but immediately after speaking of him familiarly as "*old Gay.*" How did he know he was *old Gay?* How could the warrant suggest *that* to him? But above all, how comes he to have said, "I believe that old Gay has turned

State's evidence? We all know the meaning of the term *State's evidence*: that it is used to denote an accomplice in guilt, who induced by compunction or hope of favor turns and testifies against his confederates. What does it, thus used by Fitch, mean, or intend, save an expression of belief that Gay, cognizant of their mutual guilt, had divulged his knowledge to the Government? It is idle to say that the warrant could ever have suggested to an innocent mind the idea that a stranger to him and his doings had turned State's evidence. You have seen the warrant; it simply recites the fact, and afforded the information, that the prisoners were arrested on the complaint of Henry Phelps, charging Geo. W. Gay with the arson of the Depot, and the rest of defendants in legal language as accessories before that fact.

Again, I might remark that there is no evidence, that either prisoners or officers in the car, at that time knew of the arrest of Gay. He was arrested in Detroit after the officers had gone to Leoni for these defendants, and simultaneously with them.

The truth of the narrative of Dr. Hahn is not denied. And what is the effect on a candid mind of this testimony of Clark and Hahn? In the presence and hearing of the former, Fitch says he did *not know* Phelps; before the latter, that he knew Phelps *slightly* before he went to State's Prison—since then, he knew but little about him."

And yet, Sheeley saw him cordially shaking hands with Phelps in Detroit. Doane saw him waiting for his friend from the country.

Clark testifies thus: "I was at Lansing last winter, as member of the Legislature; saw Abel F. Fitch there two or three weeks; saw Henry Phelps there about two days, while Fitch was there: P. was there twice; saw Phelps and Fitch together in the bar of the house; the next morning after P. arrived, they were sitting together talking over an hour, and once, for 15 or 20 minutes."

And Charles White says: "I remember Fitch's being in this city last winter, in February; saw Phelps here at the same time; remember the morning Phelps left on the cars, west; I saw him and Fitch together at the depot before he left, in conversation, until the cars started; saw them two or three times together that morning talking privately. Think Fitch took Phelps by the hand as they parted. Saw them together again, 18th of February, on the cars west of Dexter, going west; they talked together in a private manner, until Phelps got off at Francisco's; think the car might have been half full. Don't remember of seeing them together on any other occasion."

Gentlemen, did Fitch not know Phelps at all, or but slightly? I have been thus full in my detail of the evidence on this point, as I think it will satisfactorily answer several queries which naturally occur to our minds.

What was the bond of union between Henry Phelps and Abel F. Fitch, who claimed to have been so much his superior in wealth, rank and condition? Why these long interviews, these private talks, the anxiously expected meetings, and cordial greetings? Why, in the hour of arrest, should Fitch thus deny knowledge of Phelps, whom it is so certain he knew, and knew well? Why any falsehood at all on the subject? The theory of this case, put by the prosecution and followed up by the testimony, *alone* reconciles all these things.

Gentlemen, you must remark how naturally the words fell from the lips of Fitch, concerning old Gay, as described by Dr. Hahn. He asked to see the warrant, and it was handed to him; he saw "*he was implicated with a certain Mr. Gay, for burning the Depot.*" His first impulse was to deny that he knew him, and *he did* deny it. He paused; his head dropped; peril, danger, gloom, swept across him: his strong nerves for a moment shook, and his heart quivered; and forgetful of all present, mindful only of the tempest which had burst upon him, agony wrung from his lips, "*I believe old Gay has turned State's evidence;*" my accomplice in guilt, to save himself, has betrayed our secrets, and the avenger is upon us.

You will not forget, gentlemen, that Dr. Hahn testifies also, that as Freeland, G. Filley, and another defendant were seated together, one of them, with a bitter threat against Phelps, declared that he, after spending the winter with them as a friend, "had now *exposed the whole matter.*" It is only needful to ask, *what matter?* None other than that testified by him, is pretended to have existed between them.

You cannot fail to see, how consistent, natural and perfect, all these declarations are, with each other; with the testimony of Phelps; and with the guilt of the defendants. You cannot fail to perceive that they are inconsistent with any other hypothesis.

Gentlemen, the evidence of such declarations, from the lips of the defendants themselves, made so naturally yet so unexpectedly, placed before you by witnesses whose truth is not even questioned, must impress you deeply with the truth, that the guilty often furnish the most cogent arguments for their own conviction. In the language of an elementary and philosophical writer: "Fortunntely for the interests of society, crimes, especially those of great enormity and violence, can rarely be committed without affording vestiges by which the offender may be traced and ascertained." These vestiges sometimes come from the wrung spirit in the hour of fright or despair.

I have now, gentlemen, passed over the entire of this cause. I trust I have done so with fairness and candor. I have presented to you the case of the prosecution, and the case of the defense. Here, gentlemen, I will ask you to pause for a moment, and review with a rapid, but not careless glance, the entire testimony and cause which await your consideration and decision.

The prosecution has proved—

1. By several witnesses, whose truth is unquestioned, that a fearful combination existed between these defendants, the object of which was to injure the Railroad Company, destroy its property and burn its depots; and that in pursuance of it, many destructive and terrible outrages were committed.

2. By Wescott, whose truthfulness has been made manifest, that

the burning of the Detroit Depot, was embraced in the design of the conspiracy.

3. By experts and others acquainted with the building, its machinery, and the precautions taken, that the fire was not the result of accident.

4. By Phelps and Lake, that several of these defendants admitted that the depot was burned by Gay, and that they hired and procured him to commit the arson.

5. By a number of witnesses whose truth is not questioned, we have proven acts done, and declarations made, by these defendants, which powerfully corroborate the testimony of Phelps, Lake and Wescott, are entirely inconsistent with the innocence of defendants, and utterly irreconcilable upon any other hypothesis than their guilt, and the truthfulness of the testimony of Phelps, Lake and Wescott.

Such is the case made by the prosecution—it has traced these defendants from their first hostile feeling, through their incipient aggressions, and onward, through darkening and increasing crime, down to the perpetration of the final act, for which they are now arraigned. A case more conclusive, more perfect in its details, or more firmly knit, by corroborations of evidence and facts than that, proven against these defendants, cannot well be conceived. And how has this case been answered by the defence?

1. It was *claimed* that no conspiracy existed; but not a witness was called to sustain the proposition.

2. It was *claimed* that the instrument with which, it was alleged Gay committed the arson, was incompetent to effect that purpose; but a few hurried experiments demonstrated that for such purpose, it was so perfect and well designed, that science and skill could suggest no improvement.

3. It was *claimed* that Phelps and Lake were the manufacturers of the match; but we heard not a particle of testimony that could lead the mind towards such a conclusion; but, much that forced the conviction that they were entirely ignorant of its nature and construction.

4. It was *claimed* that Phelps and Lake carried the Niles match to the centre; but a view of the localities mentioned, the demeanor of the witnesses and a scrutiny of their testimony, revealing its improbabilities, inconsistences and contradictions, force the mind to the painful conclusion, that they swore falsely.

5. It was *claimed,* that Wescott was impeached by contradictions; but the alleged contradictions faded before the light of the testimony.

6. It was *claimed* that Phelps was impeached by evidence of general character; but you have seen that the impeachment was little better than a farce.

7. It was *claimed,* that he was impeached by contradictions; but a fair examination of the evidence showed that on every material point the contradiction was visionary.

8. It was *claimed* that he entertained malice against Phelps; but of the only two witnesses, called to prove a word or act, to indicate it, during the two years and a half he lived in his neighborhood; one

fled the state without waiting for cross examination, the other came before you, and confessed that his charges against Phelps were false and that he was suborned to make them, by a friend of the defendants. Such gentlemen, is the case of the people, and such is the case of the defendants.

I have given but a hurried outline, I have not stopped to recapetulate at length the points made or disposed of; under other circumstances, and before a different jury this might be requisite, but I am mindful of the close attention, you have given to the evidence, and the arguments; that you have in your hands printed copies of the testimony, and that you are familiar as the counsel engaged with the points, positions, progress, and facts of this case. I felt assured, as I travelled over it with you, that the same train of reasoning, and thought which forced my mind to conviction, must impress itself in yours. I felt it was not probable, scarcely possible, that you could avoid the conclusion beyond every reasonable doubt, that there existed at Leoni, a band of conspirators, whose minds were united in wreaking vengeance, and devising schemes of wickedness of every kind, and hue against the Michigan Central Railroad Company, and whose hands were employed by day and by night, in maturing that vengeance, and carrying those schemes into overt acts of the nature and extent of those in proof before you. You surely must be satisfied, that the Depot was burned by Gay, as charged in the Indictment; that burning depots was within the scope of combination of defendants; that these defendants had the disposition to have procured or incited the commission of this arson; that they were cognizant of it; and some of them accessory to the commission of the felony before the fact. But who of them are so identified and connected with the distinct felony here charged, as to justify us in requiring a verdict at your hands against them. I will endeavor *here* gentlemen to be careful, certain, and impartial. These defendants are strangers to me. I only know them as defendants in this cause, and through and by the testimony in it. I have neither motive or disposition to deal harshly with one, at the expense of another.

I know it is necessary to place before you the connecting link; that you must see and believe that not only were these defendants members of the conspiracy evidenced by the witnesses; not only that they were engaged in the depredations and unlawful acts in proof, but that they also advised, hired, incited, commanded or procured the principal felon to do and commit the felony charged in the indictment.

And in looking over the list of defendants, and the testimony against each of them, I find it to be the truth, and hence I candidly state it, that in reference to some of these prisoners, against whom there is a long and dark catalogue of crimes, who are deeply and intimately connected with the conspiracy against the road, and with the overt acts which were perpetrated for its ruin; there is yet wanting the single connecting link with the overt act presented in this indictment. That as to several others, a conviction might be legitimately asked for, but still, not with that certainty which would entirely satisfy the mind.

And again, that as to others, whose age, or other circumstances, are calculated to excite compassion, we dare not indulge it to any practical extent, in our official capocities, so fatally "has the web been woven around them.

I propose, gentlemen, to deal frankly by you, and present you first the names of those for whom, under the law and the evidence there can be no escape, save at the sacrifice of justice. Secondly, of those whom you may or may not find guilty, as you are impressed with the facts; and as to the rest, I freely concede they are entitled to your verdict.

This I do subject to your own revision, and to the exercise of your own better judgment.

I submit then, that the following twelve are marked, fixed and concluded—Ammi Filley, Lyman Champlin, Willard W. Champlin, Erastus Champlin, Eben Price, Richard Price, Orlando D. Williams, William Corwin, Ebenezer Farnham, Andrew J. Freeland, Erastus Smith, and Aaron Mount.

I hold in my hand a careful and truthful abstract of the evidence bearing against each of them, which I will hastily run over, as it will serve to freshen yonr memories, and show briefly, but distinctly, the facts which exist in the testimony against these unfortunate men, respectively.

(Mr. Van Dyke here read a compilation from the evidence adduced, of the character above proposed, and then proceeded:)

You will thus see, Gentlemen, that these twelve, are clearly criminal; that they belonged to the combination; that they were animated by dire vengeance against the Company; that they aided and assisted in many of the outrages against its rights, properties and interests; that the proofs of their guilt, are thick and fast stamped upon almost every page of the book of our evidence, and detailed by almost every one of our witnesses, who testified on this branch of the case. And you observe too, that in each and every one of their cases, it is by direct proof shown you, that they *knew of the arson of the depot*, justified the deed, *admitted they had contributed to have it done*, and thus, within every principle, legal and moral, are shown to be accessories before the fact to that Felony.

As to Minor T. Laycock, John Ackerson and Daniel Myers, I have already, in the course of my argument, and in the process of passing over the abstract just read in your hearing, given you the evidence against them, pointed out its pertinency and strength, and the little which is required, if anything, to amount to legal certainty, and to come up to the requirements of the legal rule here applicable. I submit them to you with the remark, that as to this particular offence, their cuuse is not so free from doubt, as that of the first named twelve, but that *it is* of that character which requires careful investigation before a decision either way. As to the remainder, I am glad you can conscientiously say, "Go and sin no more." Would to Heaven we dare say it to all, but the violated laws of the land, call on you for vindication, and Justice demands that the guilty be punished.

And now Gentlemen, I will not longer dwell upon the facts of this case. Aware of the long delays, and the unfortunate vicissitudes which have so marked it: aware of your intelligence, your calm yet fixed determination to do right, and of your familiarity with every fact and theory in it, I will leave it with you, without the many other suggestions, views, and arguments which have occurred to me.

If what has already transpired to convince you, I am free to think and say, nothing I could add further, would be likely to produce such effect. The law applicable to the case, gentlemen, you will receive from the able, learned and impartial judge, who, amid all the trying incidents of this case, has exhibited so much kindness, care, and patience. May I not for you and for all, tender to him, our most grateful acknowledgements.

My theme, then, is at an end. Most gladly do I divest myself of the responsibilities and burdens of this most weighty, and important trial. And oh! how cheerfully do I transfer them to a jury who of all others I have ever seen empannelled, will be most likely to dispose of them with equal and exact justice.

I have tried to do my duty, I cannot hope to have accomplished it with eloquence, power ingenuity, or distinguished ability. I have had no months or days to prepare a reply, or to write an essay; and if my humble remarks ever find their way to the world, they must go forth with but little preparation.

But if I succeeded in going over the case carefully, fairly, truthfully and with fidelity to you, to this court, and to my country; if I have aided you in wading through this mass of evidence, to perceive the truth as it is; if I have succeeded in unrobing sophistry of its artful guise; in rectifying mistakes which would lead to error; in disarming elaborate preparation of its most ingenious but most unsubstantial theories; if I have assisted yonr minds ts a clear, fair, and logical preseption of the right, and towards a just and proper conclusion, then I am happy indeed, and far more than rewarded for my labor.

Gentlemen; I feel the solemnity and importance of the place, and the hour. The long months which we have been in this Court House, are dwindled down to a span. A narrow space intervenes between us and the long looked for end. I nced not say how important it is for these prisoners :—Solitute or society, liberty or bondage tremble within the fleeting moments; and it makes me sad, to feel and believe, as I do, that the dark shadows of the prison house, are already gathering around them.

But gentlemen, there is an importance beyond the fate of these prisoners, and the limits of this court room. This cause has spread through the confines of our State and beyond its limits, and a world is looking on to see if there is here strength, and virtue sufficient to assert the integrity of the law.

The dignity, the honor, and the character Michigan are in your keeping. I feel proud and secure in knowing them there. I feel assured that when the future historian makes out the record of our past, and the pencil of truth writes down the dark details of lawless violence, and banded crime which stain our annals, and blacken our fame, there shall be written beneath it in living light, these words, which will illumine the darkness and remove the stigma: "a firm and able judge: an intelligent and honest jury, unawed by fear and prejudice, and unawed by threats, vindicated the violated law."

We are called upon by every high consideration which can induce action, to do our duty in this case. Gratitude for the lovely heritage God has given us; Patriotism, love for the beautiful peninsula, in which is fixed our destiny, and centred our all of earthly good and hope; the desire we have for her future prosperity and illustrious career, all unite in one voice, and ask that you be firm, free, and steadfast on this occasion. For if these dangerous doctrines which produce the outrages we are considering, are to be spread from the hamlets of Leoni, throughout the breadth of the land, and even to the jury box of our courts; if men animated by deep hate against a corporation, feel and think that they are justified in redressing their own real, or fancied wrongs, in their own way; if courts are to be scouted at, law trampled on, order rushed into wild confusion, and crime sympathized with, and left to stalk unpunished; then indeed have evil days come upon us. Capital, virtue, peace, and property will be trodden over, and crushed by mob violence, and all the dire evils which will follow in its train.

The first Jury which renders a verdict, tainted by the unhallowed spirit of fear, or public opinion, or prejudiced by loud clamors against monopolies and tyrannical corporations, will have stricken a death blow at his country's honor and welfare. The first Juryman who renders his verdict, in the midst of turmoil, excitement, and prejudice, unmoved by all such elements, with his conscienc impressed by his oath; with his mind calmly but deeply imbued with the truth, and regulated by the law, presents a moral spectacle, to be admired, honored and forever remembered; his action adds to the security of the commonwealth, and gives new guaranty of its perpetration.

Gentlemen: I do not intimate that there is any great volume of prejudice or passion arrayed against the Michigan Central Railroad Company. I believe that the mass of our citizens regard it as a public benefit; a mighty source of unnumbered blessings to Michigan, and its superintendants, and managers, as liberal, just and honest. Be this as it may, I do know, that Michigan is loyal to the Union and the laws. May she remain so forever! I would fain carve the sentiment on the columns of her Capitol. I would stamp it on her broad banner. I wonld wave it aloft, that her law-loving and law-abiding people might gaze on it with pride and pleasure—knowing and feeling that tney and all they have or cherish will ever find security, peace, and happiness, beneath its ample folds.

So may it be, and if so, we will soon find the State of our pride leaping on to greatness like a young giant, glowing all over with honor, vigor, and prosperity, till she becomes lustrious as the starlit sky.

But, gentlemen, fraught with importance as I deem this case to be, to the character and welfare of Michigan, still we wish no verdict at the unjust condemnation of a single citizen. Whatever your verdict may be, this prosecution, and a good community, will, and must be satisfied with it. All we required was a fair, impartial, trial; that has been obtained, and, whatever be the result, we will never murmnr against it. We know the care and anxiety it has cost you, and the inconvenience and loss it has entailed upon you. We know the consciousness you have of your weighty responsibility, and that even now you would gladly pass the cup from you. But, gentlemen, the DUTY of a good citizen, if well discharged, however painful in the present, becomes, through all after time, an abiding source of pure pleasure.

May I, for a moment, change this scene; take you to the Capitol of your Union, and turn back the tide of time, a few short months. See, there, before you, the scene of a Patriot Soldier's death bed! His life has been spent in the service of his country. His honer, like his own good sword, is without a stain. He once was exposed to the perils of this north-western frontier. He braved danger and death amid the everglades of Florida. On the terrible fields of Mexico, he bore aloft the glorious flag of our Union, graced it with new triumph and "Planted fresh stars of glory there!" The voice of a grateful nation called him to the high place of our country. But, here for him is the end of life. He has fought his last battle; he yields to the victor—Death; his eye, once gleaming through the smoke of battles, is dim; his voice, once heard like the bugle, over the clash and shouts of a deadly strife, can only whisper; and his brave heart, which never beat with fear, is flickering in its last pulsations. What do we hear now? What memories of brave deeds now come back to light up the gloom of the dark hour? What rays of earthly glory now shed their radience to cheer the dying Hero, through his last struggle? Alas! illustrious though his deeds; bright though his fame; all, all seem quite forgotten, but there does come whispering to his sinking spirit, a kindly thought, and a sweet solace, and you hear it falling tremulous from his lips: "I have endeavored to do my duty."

Gentlemen, may we endeavour to do our duty in this case, and through life, and be consoled by the reflection thereof in Death.

And now, though through with all I have to say; though happy to feel that I need no longer detain you, I yet linger ere taking my seat.

We have come together so often; we have associated in this cause so long; we have participated in our several capacitees for so many months, in all the excitements and incidents of this trial; the kindly greetings of recurring morns; the familiar faces, the pleasant intercourse, all have flung remembrances over the past, which now at the moment of parting, cluster so fresh and warm around us, that I hesitate to end them

I would fain say a word of kindness to all engaged in this cause, but it may not be appropriate to speak individually of each. I feel I may, however, with propriety allude to the Prosecuting Attorney of this County, who before you and the people he represents, has discharged his trying duties with an impartiality, ability, and fidelity, which has gained for him an enviable name.

And now for yourselves allow me to say, I cannot by words, show my high appreciation of you and your services. I can only thank you warmly and truly. May long life and every prosperity repay you for your cares and sacrifices in this cause, and when the summons comes for you to appear before the high Tribunal of another world, may each one of you with a conscious sense of duty well discharged,

——"Sustained and soothed
By an unfaltering trust, approach thy grave
Like one who wraps the drapery of his couch
About him, and lies down to pleasant dreams."

www.ingramcontent.com/pod-product-compliance
Lightning Source LLC
LaVergne TN
LVHW021417110826
845150LV00007B/1959

9781425509880